CRIMESTOPPER

CRIMESTOPPER

FIGHTING CRIME ON SCOTLAND'S STREETS

BRYAN McLAUGHLIN

with Bob Smyth

BLACK & WHITE PUBLISHING

First published 2012
by Black & White Publishing Ltd
29 Ocean Drive, Edinburgh EH6 6JL

1 3 5 7 9 10 8 6 4 2   12 13 14 15

ISBN: 978 1 84502 496 3

A CIP catalogue record for this book is available from the British Library.

Typeset by Iolaire Typesetting, Newtonmore
Printed and bound by MPG Books Ltd, Bodmin, Cornwall

To my wife, Elizabeth, and my daughters
Debbie, Janis and Lucy

CONTENTS

1

THE CASE FOR THE DEFENCE

It was a Sunday in September 1998 and the witness who could hold the key to a jailed man's freedom was walking home from church when I approached him.

He was one of three men who'd claimed in court they'd seen the accused, Stuart Gair, at a homosexual pick-up point in Glasgow in 1989. Gair was allegedly with a man called Peter Smith at the time of a fatal stabbing that led to Smith's death two weeks later. Gair was jailed for the crime in 1989 but protested he was the victim of a shocking miscarriage of justice.

Two of the witnesses – both rent boys – had since publicly retracted their stories, claiming the police had pressurised them into lying. But my target – a respectable man whose statement would carry more weight – had refused to confess he'd committed perjury. I'd first spoken to him over a year earlier, when he'd stuck to his original story. This time I told him I'd interviewed all the other people involved and I knew his version of events just couldn't be right.

He was obviously a religious man and, as we sat in my car, I reminded him that the truth was all-encompassing. He became very emotional and then, finally, he admitted he'd lied. As he got the truth off his chest after all those years, the relief he felt was obvious.

Anxious to avoid being accused of pressuring the witness to change his story, I arranged to meet him ten days later to make a statement. It was a nervous wait – but he again outlined what he'd told me that Sunday after church. In a version of events he went on to repeat at the Appeal Court in Edinburgh, he said he only picked Gair out of an identity parade because he'd been shown his picture by police and told, 'That's the one there.'

He told me that an unnamed police officer 'took me to another room with no one else there and said that if I changed my statement he would let it be known to my parents that I was gay. I did not change my statement as I took this threat seriously. I had never seen Stuart Gair before he was pointed out to me in a photograph.'

The admission was the culmination of eighteen months of work for me. I had been asked to investigate the case by Gair's legal team. One of his lawyers had cornered me at my police retirement party in 1997 and told me he had a client who was innocent. Would I look into it as a private investigator? It's an old joke that everyone in Barlinnie Prison is innocent, so I was sceptical.

I was also in two minds about rooting around in a case where the police's conduct was being questioned. I knew some of the officers involved. But lawyers can switch between prosecution and defence roles, so I decided I could do it too. Anyway, the chance to keep my investigative muscles in shape after leaving the job was appealing. So I agreed to become a gumshoe.

I'd never heard of Stuart Gair, who was described as a drifter involved in drugs and crime. I assumed he was likely to be guilty. But my attitude changed when I tracked down a rent boy who claimed he'd seen the murder victim with his attacker – but had refused to speak up before. He assured me he had never seen Gair until he met him in prison several years after the stabbing. In a statement he gave me, he claimed, 'I am certain the person I saw with the man who was murdered was not Gair.' This was a character who had an intimate knowledge of the world of rent boys and was known to the police. He convinced me he was telling the truth.

My instincts were underlined when I spoke to a man who had claimed he'd been with Gair when the stabbing took place – but later admitted lying. He was a co-accused until he gave evidence against Gair and said he'd only told the police what they wanted to hear and had never met Gair until they were both behind bars after the murder.

He'd told cops two other people had been with him and Gair that night. One was just a first name and I couldn't find the person. He said the other was one of two members of the same family – he couldn't remember which. One of them was eliminated by the police so I went looking for the other. I found him – in an urn on a mantelpiece. He'd died after being stabbed – two years before the night he was supposed to have been with Gair and the other man. Gair's one-time co-accused was the kind of person who would tell you black is white, if that's what he thought you wanted to hear. His statement was obviously full of holes and I couldn't believe he was seen as credible.

I was also convinced by the man who could have given Gair an alibi – if only he'd been called to give evidence. This guy said he was in a hostel with Gair watching TV at the time of the stabbing. I believed him. He claimed police had tried to get him to alter his statement but he wouldn't. He said he was 'gutted' he hadn't been called to the witness box when he went to court. So much so, he claimed he swore at Gair's original lawyer when he was told his evidence – a clear alibi – 'would not have helped'.

Gair was freed on bail in 2000 while waiting for his appeal, which finally began in 2004 – nearly six years after I concluded my first crack at being a private investigator. The appeal judges heard the witnesses I'd spoken to admit they'd perjured themselves, and the police officers' denial of any wrongdoing.

But, unlike me, the judges weren't convinced by the witnesses. They believed the men weren't reliable and said the witnesses could have been put under pressure by campaigners for Gair, rather than the police, to change their stories. The judges threw out that ground of appeal in 2005.

Nevertheless, they quashed Gair's conviction in 2006 due to another appeal ground. They said a failure to disclose statements by some witnesses that varied from what they later said at trial about the identification of the assailant had deprived the defence of a 'powerful argument' about their client's innocence.

But the tragedy of the story didn't end there. The following year, Gair dropped dead of a heart attack, aged just 44. I took some comfort from the fact that I'd done my best to help him win a few short months of life with his name cleared.

I still wonder about the true story behind the killing. I suspect the real murderer was linked to a gay extortion racket. I found a highly-organised gang was operating in the area where the killing took place. Gay men who went to pick up rent boys would be threatened with violence and told their sexuality would be exposed if they didn't hand over money.

One of the blackmail gang spoke publicly in 1992, saying he feared for his life. He said a knife was used to terrorise their victims. He disappeared to London and I went looking for him. I put ads in a gay newspaper but he never contacted me and nor did any of his friends.

When he described the extortion operation, he let slip a name that I believe was crucial. It was a person who matched an early description released by the police of one of the suspects in the attack on Peter Smith. This same man was found floating in the River Clyde after apparently plunging from a bridge. Two of his associates were later jailed after admitting extorting money from gay men.

It's likely Peter Smith was a victim of extortion and that something went wrong that night, leading to his stabbing. I'm convinced people who worked in the area as rent boys at the time know the identity of the real killer.

It was distasteful to think that some members of Strathclyde Police had been accused of working to get Stuart Gair, an innocent man, banged up. It wasn't the police service I recognised after more than 30 years in the job with the force and its proud predecessor, the City of Glasgow Police. The men and women I worked with were professional and diligent and wouldn't think of bending the rules to get a case off the books. I was of the same mind.

My memories took me back to my childhood days when my early motivations for becoming a copper were formed.

2

HATS OFF TO THE FIRST DAY AND WELCOME TO THE WILD LIFE

Born into a working-class family in Glasgow in 1946, I was raised as an only child in Possilpark in the north of Glasgow. I wouldn't say it was a tough area back then but everyone of my tender years 'supported' Partick Thistle Football Club for reasons of self-preservation. Being a Thistle fan was an assurance against regular assault by marauding boys who wanted to know 'what team you supported' – a veiled way of asking what religion you were.

Thistle afforded a breathing space while you made up your mind whether the enquirer was Catholic or Protestant. A wrong analysis was fraught with danger in Glasgow. Avoiding punishment in the form of a beating, I began to learn about crime. I first heard about Glasgow's notorious Barlinnie Prison when one of my school pals proudly announced that his big brother was 'away for six months to the Big Hoose'. It sounded great to a young lad – free meals and plenty of company – but my parents were not impressed with their son's choice of playmate.

I began thinking about the boys in blue when I was aged about 10. The area reached an all-time low when a uniformed police-man was attacked and seriously injured in the lane behind the tenement building where I lived. It was the talk of the steamie around my way. Not long after, we flitted to a new housing scheme on the east side of Glasgow – Easterhouse. My family hoped crime would not be rife and I suppose it was at this point in my life that I decided to become a policeman. One day, thought the young McLaughlin, I'll help purge Glasgow of evil wrong-doers and attempt to give the Barlinnie residents even more company. As a regular church attender and member of the Boys Brigade, I felt I was well placed to be on the side of the angels. To say I was naïve is an understatement.

I left Whitehill Senior Secondary School in Dennistoun aged 15. I had several clerical jobs before joining the City of Glasgow Police on September 28, 1965. Although I probably didn't realise it then, I was signing up for an institution with a proud place in policing history. Glasgow Police was the first force in Britain, established through an Act of Parliament in June 1800 – 29 years before the Metropolitan Police in London.

Little did I know what adventures lay ahead. After five years on the beat in uniform and plain clothes, I served 27 consecutive years in the Criminal Investigation Department. I saw death and despair in its many forms and witnessed sights that no one should have to endure. I arrested housebreakers, armed robbers, rapists and killers – perpetrators of almost every class of crime. I attended over 200 murders, as cop at the door to lead detective.

I saved lives, risked my own, was threatened, physically assaulted, spat on, ended up in hospital and faced guns and knives. Despite that, I have to say I enjoyed the experience and the good times, which far outweighed the bad, and learned much about the history of my city, Glasgow, and its colourful inhabitants.

Resplendent in my new police uniform I left my family home to catch a bus to Glasgow city centre. Although I was 19, my mother insisted in waving me off. Fortunately the neighbours didn't spot her. Come to think of it, I was hoping nobody would see me! What would I do if I was asked to give directions? Or called upon to arrest a bad person? Or just asked for the time (I had forgotten my watch)? At the bus stop people glowered at me, not because I was a policeman but because the bus arrived at the stop full of passengers and the conductress was happy to allow me to get on and stand at the rear platform. No doubt she felt safer while I felt apprehensive. At least I didn't have to pay my fare. Apparently all officers travelled free.

Off the bus at George Square and intending to walk towards the suspension bridge over the River Clyde to the training school in Oxford Street, I came across my first problem. A powerful gust of wind blew my hat off and, of course, it landed in a puddle. I quickly recovered it only to have it blown off again. With my headgear now firmly stuck under my arm, I headed towards my destination.

Oh dear. On arrival the sergeant shouted at me for being improperly dressed, so onto my head it went again. He told me it had a chinstrap to solve the problem of a windy day so I put it on – leaving a black streak of mud on my face from the wet strap for the rest of the morning. All sixteen new recruits had tales to tell of their first encounter with the public while in uniform that day, including one who turned up without his hat because it had blown into a bigger puddle than mine – the River Clyde! Maybe I had accidentally joined the Keystone Cops!

The first two weeks of initial training at Oxford Street was followed by a six-week residential course at the Scottish Police College at Tulliallan in Fife, where we were taught Scots criminal law. Then we were assigned to our divisions. I headed to the Central (A Division), the busiest patch with the most officers. It covered Gorbals, an area with a name famed beyond Glasgow for its tough reputation. My beat also took in Gallowgate, Townhead and West End (the city centre). On the first two Thursdays at Oxford Street we finished early to return that evening to our new division between 7pm and 11pm, or 19.00 and 23.00 hours, as police-speak would have it.

I was escorted by a senior constable around his beat to help him deal with whatever action occurred. That first turn strolling the beat turned out to be unforgettable. My 'neighbour' – the term for your police partner – worked the Townhead section. After our basic introduction we headed up the High Street to Cathedral Street at John Knox Street and entered a police box.

Glasgow police boxes were always painted red and maintained by the GPO until a new contractor took over in 1974 and changed the colour to the blue more familiar to fans of Doctor Who's TARDIS. Inside, it was certainly not as spacious as a TARDIS. It contained only one seat, a phone (which could also be used by the public), a shelf to write reports on, a light and a heater. The iconic blue light on top of the box flashed to alert the officer on the beat to contact the divisional office by phone for any messages meant for him or the area. Contrary to what I'd hoped, it had no toilet or anywhere to prepare food.

Keys for the iron gates to enter the area that surrounded Glasgow Cathedral were kept in the box. It was the duty of the night and late-shift beat officers to check that no unauthorised entry had been made to the Cathedral, and a special journal in the police box had to be signed after the area was inspected.

It was a spooky mission and it didn't help that the October darkness was lifted somewhat by the eerie light of the full moon with the silhouette of the Necropolis cemetery – the City of the Dead – towering above us between Wishart Street and the Cathedral. I was struck with fear and apprehension as we creaked open the gate. Inside, I immediately slipped on a flat gravestone and landed on top of it, covered in a green slime-like substance. My Keystone Cops antics were continuing!

I considered myself lucky as I could have ended up beside one of the founding fathers of Glasgow as a resident of the place. I later found out that my neighbour for that evening was expected to check the area on his own but never did because he too was spooked by the atmosphere. He was a big sturdy policeman but he evidently shared my disquiet.

Townhead was full of surprises that night. A statue of King Billy (William III) on his horse was situated yards from the police box. Still calming down from my experience at the Cathedral, I got another start when I swore I saw the horse's tail move from side to side. I thought the ghosts were at work again until I was told that the horse statue was one of only a few, if not the only one, with a ball and socket part in its tail that allowed it to move in the strong wind.

My second Thursday evening jaunt was in Gorbals, renowned throughout the UK at the time as a tough area with a lot of deprivation. I'd realised that I could find myself staring down the barrel of a gun at some point in my police career, but I didn't expect it to happen as early as my second outing on the beat.

Strolling with my new neighbour, I was sure I saw a man point a handgun at us from a nearby close. Surely I was imagining it? I told the experienced cop what I'd spotted and he appeared to remain composed. He didn't look round to catch the gunman's eye but he certainly put the wind up me when he said we should quicken our step in the hope that the shooter would miss us should any bullets start flying in our direction.

Out of the firing line, I was ready to call for back-up. It took my smiling partner a while to break the news to me. The gun-toting dangerman was in fact a local 'character' who wasn't exactly the full shilling. I was relieved to hear the daft sniper's favourite hobby was to target polis in the area several times a night with his – very realistic-looking – toy gun!

On our return from training at Tulliallan, new recruits taking up street duty were obliged to do six weeks of nightshift, no matter which shift their allocated section was doing. That meant you could end up doing twelve weeks straight of tiring night-shifts before joining your own shift. I well remember the shift slots that were drummed into my memory and my body clock. Night shift was 23.00 to 07.00, late shift was 14.00 to 23.00 and earlies were 0700 to 14.00.

My first day as a newly-trained constable was with my own shift and I started at 11pm at Turnbull Street Police Office, off Glasgow Cross, only to be told I was being sent to the Gorbals office. I say 'office'. It was actually a wooden hut in Commercial Road as the new office was yet to be built. I turned up and was given an update by the Gorbals sergeant on what had been happening recently in the area. I neighboured an experienced officer with ten years under his belt. His surname was Mac-Lachlan, a different spelling from mine but one of the clan nonetheless. My second name would play an unlikely part in my first arrest that day.

We headed to a disturbance in the Rutherglen Road area where we encountered some local worthies causing a disturbance. This resulted in my first collar – a woman called Mclaughlin! I clearly remember noting her moniker when she was being charged with a breach of the peace at the station. She was taken to the cells and I swung the door shut on her, taking away her freedom until her court appearance. It was a strange feeling, having the power of arrest and using it for the first time. I recall she pled not guilty, meaning I went on to have my first experience of giving evidence in a court of law.

The hearing was at the Central Police Court before a stipendiary magistrate. His name? Would you believe it? Maclauchlan! Well, it's nice to keep it in the family.

Each of the seven divisions had three shifts. I was attached to No.2 shift, which had about 30 beat constables plus administration staff and officers of rank. Constables and sergeants had metal numbers on their shoulders which had the divisional letter (in my case A) plus the shift (2) and where you worked in the division. Low numbers signified administration while new recruits, known as probationers, had numbers from 210 to 219 for their first two years' service. The other numbers referred to the four sections within the division. I was A214 for two years then A255 for the Gallowgate area. The probationer's number meant you were 'flying' within the whole division, which allowed you to not only learn about the whole area but work with everyone in it. It was a great way to get experience as every area was different and each older cop had various degrees of ambition and experience to impart.

My first days with the shift were mainly served in Gorbals. On one occasion I was taken to the police box by my neighbour at about 4am. By that time he was bored out of his skull as very little happened in the wee small hours. It looked like he had some hunting on his mind when he produced an air-rifle. But we weren't going to aim our sights at the local baddies. It was time for some fun to kill the time.

He took me to the rear of tenements which were about to be demolished and we entered silently. Then he told me to throw a brick into the middens – the overflowing piles of rubbish. A wall separated each area of the middens and a spare brick was usually available from the crumbling structures. I lobbed my missile and watched in surprise as the garbage heap came to life.

The brick disturbed the army of rats that were gorging on the mounds of waste. They scampered up the walls and along the dyke, heading for safety. But my tutor constable had other ideas and shot as many as he could off the dyke. Our target practice passed many a happy hour during the night while almost everyone was sleeping. Fortunately, the Scottish SPCA never found out about our unlikely Pied Piper pastime.

Finally, I got a break from the night shift and did my first early start. Turned out it was an eye-opener. Having finished late shift at 11pm, I had to be in the office for a bleary-eyed quick changeover at 6.45 the next morning. Sent again to Gorbals, I neighboured a particular officer for the first time. Normal procedure for early shift was to head to the nearest place on the beat for a decent cup of tea. But today we strode purposefully to a tenement close and knocked on a door, which was opened by a sleepy man. He got quite a wake-up call! No words were exchanged and we entered the house (no mention of a warrant) of the well-known householder (code used in court for 'notorious housebreaker'). The next thing I saw, the man was lying flat out on the floor, unconscious. We left – after ensuring that he was still alive. Curious as to why we had called at the house, I asked the older, experienced cop what it was all about. Over our delayed cup of tea, he told me of an incident the previous night.

Walking on his own, he'd been threatened with violence by the man we'd just dropped in on. Two drunken pals had also joined in the baiting. My neighbour's firm belief was that he had to walk the beat, often on his own, and if he was not dominant over the local criminal fraternity he would open himself up to being assaulted. He had to have the power within his beat and respect from those who were minded to upset the fragile balance that kept peace on the streets. The householder obviously appreciated the rules and no complaint was made by him – or me. That was how things worked back then.

Getting used to night shifts, the first thing that hit me – something I'll never forget – was the moment the peace was shattered as I strolled through Glasgow Cross. It would come when a bus started in town. The city was so quiet and relatively free from traffic back then that just one vehicle switching on its engine was so deafening it nearly blew your ears. Wandering about in the daytime as traffic rushes by, everyone just assumes that noise level is the norm and they cope with it. But if, like the early-morning PC, you'd been bathed in silence, you realise just what noise pollution is in the city.

Another sound that drove me to distraction was the wail of a crying baby. I'd often hear it coming from the darkness of the back courts. But when I got there, no tot was to be found. Instead, there was always a big cat sitting on the midden, emitting the cries. Any bobby will tell you, they sounded exactly like a baby and every time you had to go out of your way to check it out – just in case it was an abandoned tot and not a moaning moggy.

There was nothing more boring than strolling about a beat at three o'clock in the morning. By then I'd already been back in for my break and I had another four hours of my shift to go. Nearly everybody was sleeping and it was too soon for the early risers to appear in town to give me something to pay attention to.

At that time a regular wheeze was to go round the local butcher's shops and peer in the windows. The reason was simple. Although they cleared all their meat from the window display overnight, they all had a decorative show of eggs lined up along the glass. Another fixture at nearly every butcher's was a cat – in case any mice appeared during the night.

To pass the time, I'd knock on the window and the cat, which was as in need of entertainment as me, would come up to greet me through the glass. Time to have some fun with puss. I'd tap my finger high up the window and animal would jump up, trying to get at it. Invariably, it would slide down the window and land on the eggs. The trick was to see how much that moggy in the window could break.

After entertaining myself with the dancing cat for a while, I'd head off. Well, you can't have fun without breaking a few eggs. The cat game was learned from older cops. When they appeared from the beat and you asked them, 'Anything doing?' they'd reply, 'Not much, but I managed to break a couple of eggs at the butcher's.' After a while it became an unofficial competition. No doubt there were a few butchers around town who wondered why they were often greeted with the sight of unwelcome scrambled eggs at breakfast time.

We had to keep our police boxes clean, so one of the japes was to booby trap them – with pigeons. The birds would be collected and crammed in the box at the end of a shift and the next guy on would open it up and be hit with a fleeing flock of birds. Then he'd have all the mess to clean up too.

There were more animal surprises to be had when I came across the city's rat population. I was on hand to witness the rodents as they moved about during the night. I once looked on in horror at a plague of them scuttling down West Nile Street in the early hours. There were scores of the usually-hidden creatures – not something you'd ever see in the daylight.

Of course, I got to know the unfortunate people who lived on the streets. The hard-drinking dossers would gather when the pubs put the empty bottles out for collection early in the morning. The down-and-outs knew there was gold in them-thar whisky bottles when the dregs collected. They were soon sucking from the discarded booze containers. One of their number was an avid newspaper reader. He wasn't catching up on current affairs, just scanning the deaths column for news of when funeral services would be held. He got his dinner regularly by inveigling himself among the grieving friends and relatives.

I realised how horrific it was to be locked up. But I also soon learned that for some it was a bonus that actually improved their standard of life. One, in particular, had a guaranteed way of getting himself a warm bed behind bars. After enjoying a bucket in the pubs, he'd stagger to Buchanan Street and put in the window of an upmarket clothes store. He'd pinch a nice suit from the display but not bother to put it on. He was keener on wearing prison stripes.

So he'd just stand and wait, suit in hand, until we arrived, unsurprised to find him there. He'd get his 60 days but not long after coming out he'd be boozed up and window shopping again. He preferred the 'first-class' accommodation of Barlinnie Prison to the service offered by the 'models', as the homeless shelters were called.

On one of my first nightshifts, the quiet of the early-morning city centre was broken by a sound that was more likely to be heard in Africa than a corner of Scotland. The roar of a lion! I thought I was imagining it. But I took on the role of big game hunter and tracked the sound up an alley.

Would you believe it! There, indeed, was a lion in a cage. The beast, located in a small yard off Oswald Street, seemed pleased enough to see me. I didn't fancy getting too close, although the animal appeared relaxed with humans. I assumed it must be a big cat from a zoo that was being stored there for a short while.

Looking back, I wonder if it was Rajah – a star at Wilson's Zoo in the city. The zoo, which was in Oswald Street and later moved to Carlton Place, was quite a talking point although I don't remember ever being taken there as a child. It was said to have had a panther at one point and a mynah bird that spoke in a Glaswegian accent and was insured for £200. It had a microphone on its cage to broadcast its chat, which included: 'Here comes the sawdust man.'

In the 1930s there was a fire at the Oswald Street building that killed a number of the 200 creatures, including monkeys, macaws, a vulture, rabbits and guinea pigs. There was a lion and a lioness in the menagerie at the time but they survived the effects of smoke and heat.

In the 1950s it was hit by crime when a man called Sherlock pinched a lovebird. But the clueless thief didn't live up to the reputation of his brainy namesake, Sherlock Holmes, and was spotted by the zoo manageress the next day wandering about with a bird cage. She'd been given a description of the thief and reckoned he fitted the bill, so she followed him home and reported him to the cops. Sherlock said he'd acted on the spur of the moment when he took the bird, later swapping it for a cage in a shop. In the tough ways of the day, he was fined £2, with the alternative of 20 days in jail, for stealing the £5 lovebird.

Rajah the lion became a fixture in the 1950s, having arrived as a cub that became used to doing its party piece for humans. Some said he was toothless when older, others said he had a full set of gnashers. The king of the city jungle loved his fans and the zoo boss, Andrew Wilson, insisted he was so friendly that folk sat on his back to be photographed. But Rajah still had an edge and he got into trouble for lashing out at a customer who was teasing him. The man patted Rajah through the bars but went too far when he pulled the lion's mane. The beast shot out a claw and caught the back of the customer's hands. Fortunately, the visitor made light of his scratched and bleeding hand, despite needing treatment at the Royal Infirmary.

In 1960 poor old Rajah was having his hair pulled by another visitor. This time it was a drunken 21-year-old who was pestering the great beast. On a Saturday afternoon Samuel Harper got up to some monkey business by climbing over the safety rail and going up to the chimps' cage. He was persuaded back but then leapt the barrier at Rajah's pen and thrust his hand into the cage. As he pulled the slumbering lion's mane, women screamed in horror. Harper insisted he knew more about lions than the attendant then got into a fight with the boss, Andrew Wilson, who'd warned him he was causing a disturbance and putting himself in danger. He grabbed the zoo owner him by the lapels and shoved him to the ground. All the noise was enough to wake up Rajah, who'd slept through the assault on his mane. Mr Wilson said the big cat was well trained but could become dangerous if abused. Harper apologised and was fined £3 or 20 days for breach of the peace and £5 or 30 days for the assault.

That same year Rajah was said to be a tired beast, aged either 19 or 25, depending on which reports you read. He had to be put under to have his claws trimmed and was apparently very groggy for a few days after the procedure. But he managed a low roar when he was brought some water after he came round.

Was the elderly jungle king I found five years later the pensioned-off Rajah? Who knows but it certainly was one of the more unusual city centre residents I encountered. And the gentle lion was probably less of a wild animal than some of the humans I had to deal with.

3

LADIES OF THE NIGHT
AND CADAVERS GALORE

I was brand new on the shift and the powers-that-be weren't going to let me loose. I was put in a car with an experienced PC and he took me round to meet all the people in A Division so I could see what was what.

My partner in the Ford Corsair was a real gentleman, who patiently showed me what I had to know. We'll call him Jim. One of these car trips with Jim resulted in the naïve young McLaughlin's initiation into the world of Glasgow's prostitutes. I was taken up to Blythswood Square in the city centre, which was a hotbed of illicit goings-on.

The women there were at the top end of the pecking order for street girls, charging £5. That was a lot of money. They would take the punters back to an upmarket hotel or a flat they had – so everything was all laid on, so to speak!

Then you moved down the scale to the £3-a-time girls. They were the ones who were not as attractive as those up at Blythswood Square were, or believed themselves to be. These cheaper 'hoors' usually sneaked up the lanes with their customers. There were plenty of suitable dark alleys for a swift, soulless encounter around the area. Sometimes they would go to a downmarket hotel or even the man's car, but at that time not many of the punters had vehicles. Then you had the bottom end of the scale – the women who had sunk right down and had been reduced to charging a pound for a knee-trembler.

As we drove round the area, Jim was pointing them all out to me. He indicated a well-known trio – Mary, Maggie and Jeannie, all of them in their mid-thirties. He gave them a wave and we continued on our round to see what else was going on.

Later, we rolled back around and saw the three women were still on their beat, too. But this time Mary and Maggie were doubled-up laughing, and Jeannie was obviously not a happy bunny at all. Clearly, something had happened and we couldn't resist stopping to find out what.

Jim rolled down the window to get the full story. Through their tears of laughter the chortling duo filled us in. Jeannie, who had been a £3 girl until just recently, was having difficulty adjusting to her new ranking and thought she was too good for the £1-a-time market.

When a punter had come up to the trio and asked how much, Jeannie had jumped in before the other two had a chance to sell their wares. She'd chanced her arm and offered herself for £3.

Somewhat to the surprise of her disgruntled pals, the man had agreed and they had disappeared up the lane. The punter had handed over a fiver and Jeannie had given him change of two pound notes. The business had been transacted and Jeannie had left the lane into the better light.

At this point she'd stopped in her tracks, realising she'd been stung. The man had slipped her a 'Chinese fiver' – the term for a foreign note or dud money. Her two colleagues were in stitches because she'd got her comeuppance for overcharging. Her quick action to scoop up the punter had, in the end, cost her £2 for giving the man sex.

But Jim decided to have some fun with the situation. He told the girls, 'I wouldnae be laughing if I was you because foreign notes can be worth a fortune. I know a lot about numismatics.' His mention of such an impressive-sounding understanding of money wiped the smiles off the faces of Maggie and Mary. Jeannie was now hanging onto Jim's arm through the window. 'Do you think it's worth an awful lot, constable?' she pleaded.

So he put the light on in the car and he made a play of looking at the note for a while, claiming he was trying to spot crucial features, a watermark and the like. Her excitement reached a peak as she tugged on his arm for a valuation of her foreign booty. 'I'll just turn it over and check,' he explained. Then his voice took on a mock tone of disappointment. 'Oh! No, sorry, it's not got what it should have on this side to be make it valuable.'

'How much is it worth then, officer?' she demanded. Jim delivered his punchline with expert timing. 'Sorry, Jeannie, your fiver's no' worth a f***.' His quip left me unable to move for laughing and Jeannie's friends were hooting once more. That was my first taste of the humour among the pain and heartbreak on the streets.

There was another laugh later when I was more accustomed to the red light district. One nightshift I was trudging the chilly streets. There was frost on the ground and the city was quiet. As I've said, sound really travels during the peaceful nights so I was intrigued by a noise in the distance. It sounded like someone kicking a tin can. But it went on for a surprisingly long time so I decided to check out exactly what was happening.

I walked round the corner of a street near Blythswood Square and was met by an unlikely sight. Four of the girls were on the game – of a different sort. They were playing football, booting about a tin can in their heels. The cold night meant there weren't many punters cruising for action, so the hoors were keeping warm by improving their tanner ba' skills. They normally chucked their night's work around 2am so I guessed the big match was helping them kill time while business was slack, so to speak.

It wasn't jumpers for goal posts, it was handbags that were either side of the goalie. Three of them were competing for the 'ball', dribbling up and down in the finest traditions of the impish Scottish winger. The young woman who was in the role of keeper was leaping about animatedly as she tried to stop the flying can from going between the posts.

I sauntered up to have a blether.

'Playing football?'

'Yes,' said the keeper. 'I'm the goalie. And, by the way, I'm the best ever goalie.'

Her pals smiled knowingly but, like a fool, I replied, 'How's that?'

'Because I let everything in bar the balls,' she answered as quick as a flash. The quiet of the early morning was shattered again, this time by peals of laughter from me and the girls.

I learned that the prostitutes were normal human beings who had fallen on hard times. They did what they had to do for the money. Some had to pay for drink and a 'stick man' – a pimp, who protected them – but drug addiction wasn't such a driver for street workers then.

We had a tremendous amount of dealings with them and I certainly felt very sorry for some of them. They became useful sources of information as they knew what was happening on the streets. Of course, we could charge them with certain acts, such as loitering with the intention of prostitution. But that wasn't always the most sensible move. They were good informants, they were going to come back despite being prosecuted and they could be driven underground if we were heavy-handed with them.

So there was an unofficial system in terms of arrest. It was something like a rota, telling them, 'It's your turn to get nicked next week.' It was done by the dayshift boys, who normally did the parking enforcement. Four of them were taken off their regular beat to become the 'hoor squad'. They did a week of 6pm to 2am shifts to control the red light area and ensure the arrest figures were up. That helped counter the numerous complaints made by female office workers on their way home in the area. They were often accosted by kerb crawlers in cars and on foot.

The red-light squad could have cleared all the prostitutes in one night but that would have been totally impractical. It would have clogged up the cells. Efforts were made to shift the girls to another, less-populated area, which would not attract the same complaints, but to no avail. However, a way to move them was eventually found – build a big police station beside them.

Today there are no prostitutes in Blythswood Square, thanks to the formation of Strathclyde Police in 1975. A new police headquarters was located in the city's Pitt Street, which is one street down from Blythswood Square. The street girls scarpered to other shady corners of the city after that, reckoning the new cop shop was too close for comfort for them and their customers.

Among the Blythswood Square girls, one ruled the roost for a while. Jane had come north from England when she was only 18. All the punters were interested in Jane because she was such a looker. If you saw her, the last thing on your mind would be that she was a prostitute. She was like a model and caused quite a sensation, allowing her to charge what the heck she wanted.

I bumped into her regularly while patrolling the beat in the centre of town. She was a chatty, self-confident type, in rude health, if you will. If she was addicted to anything, I couldn't tell. Eventually she disappeared off the face of the earth and I assumed she'd gone back south. She turned up again a couple of years later. She had indeed been in England – but her move had been a bad decision.

It took me a minute to recognise her on her return. Whatever had happened since I'd last seen her, she had been through a nightmare. Still in her early twenties, she had a scar from ear to lip, a broken nose, teeth missing and a tortured look in her sunken eyes. Gone was the head-turner of a few years before.

In truth, she'd become a complete wreck. She told me she'd been assaulted by customers, a permanent threat in her dangerous line of work. I suspected she'd been abusing the booze as well. I was struck by her sad situation. In a short period of time she'd become a physical wreck and was heading for life as one of the down-and-outs I dealt with every night.

Jane, the queen of Blythswood Square, was now a £1-a-time prostitute. It was sad to see a well-adjusted girl who appeared to have been properly brought up slump so low. I don't know what became of her after I stopped walking the beat in that area but I suspect she didn't live very long.

Not all of the prostitutes were regulars. Sometimes we had an unusual collection of women on the street we'd never seen before. Whenever there was a big football match at Hampden Park, the influx of supporters also brought in a flood of part-time hoors. By day they were respectable housewives but the football bonanza lured them into the twilight world of prostitution to boost the housekeeping money. They counted on no-one recognising them.

Others had regular jobs but still needed the extra cash. One who stands out in my memory was a primary school teacher, who was in her early twenties. When I noted it was unusual to find a teacher on the street, Miss asked me, 'Do you think it's awfully mundane of me?'

Then there were the transvestites. Some came out in the late hours just to be able to wander about dressed as women under cover of darkness. Others became working 'girls'. They would con the punters into thinking they were real women who were unable to do the full business for whatever reason, such as time of the month. But they would perform other acts on the unsuspecting clients.

Other customers were well aware they were with a man in a frock. I well remember the conversation I had with the wife of a guy we'd arrested for sodomy, which was a serious crime back then. A cop had been sent to her door to alert her but had got no response. We phoned several times and finally got hold of her about 3am. When I told her I was a police officer, she immediately said, 'Is it about my husband? Is he by any chance dressed as a woman?' She then described the female clothing he was wearing and lamented her situation. 'I've suspected for a while but I don't know what to do,' she said. I didn't know what to tell her.

There was an overflow of English sex workers in the 1970s. They'd come to the mean streets of Glasgow to escape the even more frightening threat of the Yorkshire Ripper, who murdered 13 women, mostly prostitutes. It was interesting to hear so many Yorkshire accents in the city's red light areas.

From well-known footballers, to ministers, priests, sheriffs, senior legal figures and cops, I saw them all getting mixed up with vice. One man of the cloth had a very strange kink, which involved the girls filling a balloon in an unusual way. At one point an informer whose partner was on the game handed me a driving licence that had been filched from the clothing of a client, no doubt along with his wallet. It turned out to belong to a very senior policeman who was about to retire. I popped it in the force's internal mail system and said no more about it. Another time a top cop from another force was caught with a prostitute – a male one.

If punters were robbed by a hoor or their stick man, they were unlikely to report it. I once recovered a fancy watch from a prostitute's house. It was top-of-the-range Rolex and was valued at £4,000 – a lot of money now, never mind back then in the early 1980s. She admitted she'd got it off a punter who'd never alerted the police, so it was sent to an auctioneer's and the money went into the council's Common Good Fund.

As a probationer I became involved in the seedy world of Glasgow's vice trade. I was a fresh-faced youth so I fitted the bill when senior officers needed someone to make an undercover visit to the city's first sex shop. Unlike these days, they weren't licensed to sell the explicit porn they stocked.

The dirty book store was in Cunningham Street and I was given a fiver and told to go and get some eye-popping evidence to prosecute the owner. I sheepishly slipped into the premises, which had a regular bookshop at the front and the sex shop at the rear. If you furtively asked for something from under the counter, the boss would look you over and take you into the back to peruse the goods.

It was a dark and dingy place, illuminated by candles, with rows of porn publications on the shelves. I wasn't familiar with such material but my job was to find the dirtiest thing I could uncover so we could later go back with a warrant and raid the place. I decided to grab something and get out of there quickly. As I leaned forward to pick up a magazine, my arm came into close proximity to one of the candles. 'Don't cook your goose, son,' smirked the sleazy book salesman.

I plucked a highly-explicit publication from his collection. It was called 'Coloured Sex No.42' and featured an athletic black man with a white woman. At my age, it was quite incredible to behold. The strongest material we had was *Health and Efficiency* magazine!

Glad to get out of the sleazy environment, I headed to see the stipendiary magistrate to get the warrant. I introduced myself and he held his hand up and made me swear an oath. I explained why I was there, outlining my visit to the store.

As he munched on a sandwich and slurped his tea, he asked to see the evidence of obscene material. I placed 'Coloured Sex No.42' on his desk and he nearly choked on his lunch. He silently leafed through the magazine and declared there was undoubtedly enough evidence. 'I grant you a warrant,' he declared. Then he paused and, with a cheeky smile, added, 'Gonnae hurry up and get me Coloured Sex No.43!' We had a good laugh and the cops got a lot more than that when we raided the shop and confiscated the huge porn collection.

Early in my career I was sent to a 'model' as the homeless hostels were called. They were supposed to be a model example of how such lodging houses should be and, in local rhyming slang, were called 'deedle doddles'.

A possible death was reported at the model and an ambulance was on the way to the scene. When I arrived I looked around but saw no sign of a body on the floor or lying on a bed. I asked where the corpse was and a member of staff indicated with a casual wave of the hand.

All I could see was a table of four of the residents, playing cards. I looked around the place in confusion as I approach them and asked if they knew anything about a guy who was ill or had collapsed. I was astonished when three of them indicated the fourth member of the card school. Right enough, he was pretty quiet. He was sitting there with his cards in his hand but he was glassy-eyed and pale. As the game went on around me I checked him and couldn't find a pulse.

It seemed incredible but his pals had carried on playing after he'd passed away in front of them. He was only in his thirties. Not wanting to disturb the body, they had opened a new pack of cards and kept going while he sat there with the best poker face in history.

The boss of the place didn't seem too concerned and was just anxious to get the body moved out. Maybe he had another resident needing the space. The ambulance crew arrived and we took him to the Royal Infirmary just in case there was anything that could be done for him. But the way his head bounced about in the back of the emergency vehicle told its own story – he was long gone. He was classed by the medical staff as a 'DOA' – Dead on Arrival – and taken to the City Mortuary. For the young homeless guy it was definitely a case of unlucky at cards.

Trips to the mortuary are always difficult. It's traumatic to see your first dead body but even more so when they've lost their lives in appalling circumstances.

When I took the dead card player to the mortuary, feeling bold and nosy, I made the mistake of asking the attendant if he had any 'good' bodies in. He had 15 corpses on trolleys or in the drawers. I looked on in increasing horror as he pulled back the white sheets and showed me.

There was a frighteningly-burned victim of a fire, someone who'd lost their legs in a car accident, a murder victim who'd been stabbed and slashed and a dead child. I didn't want to see the others. I was still living at my parents' home at the time and, when I arrived at the house that night, my mother saw I was pale and shaken. She wasn't much for drinking but she poured me a whisky to calm my nerves.

As a detective I had to attend a catalogue of gruelling post-mortems. Next time you see a senior CID man on the telly appealing for information in a murder case just remember he has good reason to look a bit frazzled. He's probably been up all night investigating the crime and witnessing a graphic autopsy on the victim.

I was always astounded by the blasé attitude of the medical staff who did the PMs but I suppose they we so used to it they weren't affected. I'll never forget the two female staff who were removing bullets from a body while happily talking about their lunchtime shopping trip and the latest bargains they'd scooped.

Another astonishing thing I witnessed was a man being stuffed with newspapers – like some kind of gruesome Guy headed for the bonfire. His insides had already been removed when we got word that some relatives were coming to see his body. The guts, which had been put in a sink, were accidentally chopped up in the waste disposal system so the staff had a problem. His belly looked pretty sunken without his intestines. So all the newspapers that were lying around were collected up and packed into his body cavity before he was stitched up. I suppose he must have looked alright because they got away with it. It was pretty shocking for me to see. I just hope he wasn't cremated because all that paper would have caused an unusual effect.

I once encountered a leading funeral director at the mortuary. I asked him how he coped with seeing all the bodies and the mournful aspect of his job. He admitted that earlier that day he'd had a smile on his face at a funeral. His budgie had died and he'd decided to give it a lavish send-off by popping it into a coffin that was due to be buried. He'd concealed it under the pillow where the deceased's head was resting. He said it had cheered him up to see the cortege following behind his feathered friend's coffin.

I was never much of a football fan, which turned out to be a painful mistake when I went to patrol the sidelines at Ibrox Park during a volatile Rangers-Celtic league match in the late '60s. I recall Celtic were poised to win the championship so the home fans were even more fired up than usual about seeing their team notch a victory. A huge police presence was there and I was keeping an eye on the baying crowd from the edge of the pitch as the tense drama drew to a close.

Amid the ranting fans, one man stood out because of his light-coloured top. I noticed him draining the dregs of a whisky bottle and launching it onto the pitch. Luckily, it didn't hit the players or referee. But there was a howl from the fans and the match was delayed for a moment. Keeping my eye on the hooligan I decided to go in and get him. I hoped the supporters would help me as they didn't want idiots like that in their midst.

There was a low wall in front of me and for some reason there was a gap in the terraces behind it. The best place to enter the crowd, I thought. I put my hand on the wall and sprang over it. But it was raining and the top of the wall was soaking. My hand slipped and I came crashing down on my elbow, sending an agonising pain through my arm. Worse was to come. I toppled sideways and plunged horizontally onto the ground on the other side of the wall.

The reason that no fans had been standing there suddenly became obvious. It was where a large puddle of pee had pooled thanks to supporters who couldn't get to the loo and were happy to urinate on the terraces. I found myself swimming in a sea of urine and rainwater as the crowd yelled their approval and laughed at my predicament.

As I was led away for medical help I gave my colleagues a description of the wanted man and they picked him up and gave me his details. That came in handy. After treatment at hospital for a broken elbow I was able to make a claim to the Criminal Injuries Compensation Board. Yes, even cops can get financial recompense for being hurt through a crime. My pay-out was a decent amount and helped me put down a deposit on a house.

The second time I needed treatment after an incident on duty came after a mass gang fight outside the Kelvin Hall. It was horrible to be in the middle of something like that. Knives and boulders were flying and I had no idea what could hit me next. I saw one of the neds haring about with a sword. It was the type used for sword-fencing – an epee with a long, thin blade. It could easily have done some damage so I tangled with the swordsman to disarm him. I got it off him but amid the scuffle I suffered a powerful kick to my left knee. I was left hobbling for a while and eventually had to go to hospital to get the cartilage removed. The war wound resulted in another Criminal Injuries payment. I still have the scar on my knee to this day.

Another day and another terrifying attack. The station sergeant at Gorbals got me and half-a-dozen others to help control the crowds after on Old Firm clash at Hampden Park, the national football stadium in Glasgow.

We filtered the Rangers fans down one street and the Celtic supporters along another. But at one point one group of supporters found some stones that were there because of road-works at that spot. The fans began lobbing the rocks over our heads at their football enemies. The other side picked up the missiles and threw them right back.

Then both groups took great offence at us trying to break up their violent fun. Suddenly, the old enemies bonded and found a common foe – the polis. Soon rocks were raining down on us. There were no plastic shields to protect us. It was a nightmare as we dodged the onslaught.

After they had been seen off, I was uninjured and I don't think any of my colleagues were hurt either. There wouldn't have been much sympathy for us if we had been. But it just showed how a routine police operation could flare up into something poten-tially deadly when you least expected it.

At one point we had a problem with recurring vandalism at a shop in Gorbals. A newsagent's, run by a very respectable lady, was continually having its windows punted in. Someone would creep up in dead of night and throw a brick through the large glass window, causing costly damage and putting up the fru-strated shop owner's insurance premiums.

One man was a prime suspect. He'd been in some kind of dispute with the newsagent – maybe he hadn't had his papers delivered on time! The disgruntled individual was highly likely to have been behind the spate of attacks. But he denied it and we had no witnesses or other evidence. There were about four occasions when the window was panned in but it's not easy to get fingerprints off bricks!

One night a late-shift bobby found a man lying in the street, with a head injury. A brick lay next to him. It was treated as an assault and he was taken to hospital and patched up. But next day it transpired it was the man who was chief suspect for the shop vandalism. And he'd been found on the ground outside the store.

It couldn't be coincidence. Had the shop owner or her family waited in the shadows and taken violent revenge when he'd turned up for his latest smashing time? No, it was more bizarre than that. Unknown to us, the shop boss had decided she'd take decisive action to stop her window being broken. So she'd had a plastic, reinforced pane put in. It was much less vulnerable than glass so when the annoying vandal had lobbed his brick at the window, the missile had bounced off the protective shield and flown back into his face, knocking him senseless. He certainly got what he deserved and we were able to arrest him for all the vandalism thanks to the 'pain' of plastic glass.

4

SQUARE GOES, FOOT RACES
AND CLASS DISTINCTION

The threat of getting injured or involved in a punch-up was always there and it hit home to me while I was still a novice cop and we got an alarm call from Glasgow's council bosses at the City Chambers. A man had walked into the foyer of the historic building and demanded to see someone about a problem he was having. After being told there was no one to help him he'd begun a surprise sit-in, plonking himself on a chair and refusing to budge.

The staff could do nothing to convince him to end his protest so the cops were called to shift him. I was the first to reach the scene and strolled up to him. I was in uniform so it was obvious to the man, in his forties, that I wasn't another corporation jobsworth. Being as calm and friendly as possible, I asked him what the problem was. Instead of outlining his gripes to me he moved his protest to direct action.

He leapt to his feet, picked up his chair and walloped me with it. I staggered backwards but survived the onslaught and managed to wrestle the chair from him and grab my attacker. Soon we were rolling on the floor of the distinguished surroundings and I became aware that the stushie meant we had a growing audience. More and more folk were leaning over the balcony looking down on the pair of us as if we were scrapping in a bear pit. I assume there were councillors and other local worthies among the viewers.

Realising I was being watched – although not helped – I knew I couldn't be overly rough with the madman. It wasn't an option to whack him with my baton or punch him in the jaw. But he was an exceptionally fit 40-year-old and it was tough to keep him under control. I was in a dilemma – how to contain the fired-up character who was intent on rearranging my facial features while I was being closely observed by a crowd who may or may not have been pro-police.

We continued to tangle for a while as the amused onlookers enjoyed the floorshow. Eventually, other cops arrived to help me subdue him and the City Chambers wrestling extravaganza came to an end. I never found out what his complaint was about but I wonder if it was worth a charge of assaulting a policeman.

When the last buses gathered at George Square at the weekend to ferry home the drunken clubbers there was always a risk of trouble. Gang fights were inevitable as the neds from the north met the neds from the south and the daft boys from the west encountered their counterparts from the east. Full of Dutch courage at midnight, they were spoiling for a fight.

It could become a battle royal involving scores of trouble-makers. Officers on backshift were asked to stay on to 1am while nightshift cops started early at 9pm. The neds had weapons stashed in the lanes beside the square. We went hunting for them but many were well concealed. Some of the gangs wore recognisable clothing and hats as a sort of uniform.

There was no shortage of mayhem and plenty of knives and other offensive weapons were collected by the overworked cops. Eventually, things got so bad that extra officers were drafted in. Some were a little too anxious to spring into action. At one point I saw a man with a wispy beard. Indicating his goatee, I told my colleague, 'There's a guy acting the goat.'

My neighbour obviously misinterpreted my comment and thought he'd missed the reveller getting up to some nonsense. To increase his alarm, the man just happened to sprint off for his bus at that moment. Before I could stop him the other cop was in hot pursuit. He dragged the guy off his bus and was dealing with him when I caught up and quietly informed him he'd got it wrong.

Thinking on our feet, we apologised to the reveller and told him it was a case of mistaken identity that had required quick action. Having missed his bus, the bearded chap was quite understanding. He didn't realise his goatee had been the butt of our joke.

When there were no gang fights, the city centre shop doorways and alleys weren't only crammed with amorous couples having a final winch before they went their separate ways to catch their buses home. I was amazed at how often I saw two women locked in a passionate embrace. I had no idea lesbians existed until I witnessed it for myself. I quickly realised that Glasgow was home to a large lesbian community.

The George Square carnage began to subside over the years as more people got their own cars or earned enough to take a taxi home. I remember getting my first car in 1971 and it's interesting to think how modern technology can change patterns of behaviour.

Around that time I used to drop in on a wee newsagent's shop in Townhead for a cup of tea on the early shift. I always chatted to the owner and got to know him quite well. One day I found a note from him in the police box. He wanted me to pop up to the shop because he needed some help. When I arrived he told me the local Catholic church had need of my services. Turned out a sneak thief had been going in there on Sundays and pinching the cash in the offertory box – money that had been donated by the congregation. It was a particularly despicable crime.

The priest had apparently narrowed the suspects down to a man in his forties who arrived by bus early on a Sunday morning and would go into the church to pray. But after his visits the box would be broken into. Could I go and keep any eye on things, the shopkeeper wondered? It was a Saturday so I said I'd go up later and get details from the priest then have a look in at the church the following morning.

But events overtook me as I sat there munching my piece at breakfast. In a scene that reminded me of the speeded-up chase sequences in the Benny Hill comedy show, a man in his forties was dashing down the street. He was pursued by at least ten members of the congregation, including three middle-aged matrons from the chapel. Two priests, wearing their smocks, were also sprinting behind him. The large cross worn by one of the two fathers was swinging wildly around his neck as he went at full pelt.

I had to join in and soon caught up with the priest. 'Is this the guy who's been stealing from the offertory box?' I asked.

'Yes,' he peched, as I tore ahead.

It was a busy area and the locals must have had a good laugh as they watched the comical procession. At one point a double-decker bus passed along Castle Street. It was packed with people who were staring out of the windows in amazement. It must have been the highlight of their day. My youth and fitness meant I caught the penny-pinching thief and he was duly arrested for his filching of church funds. The exhausted clergy were delighted to have had the problem sorted out.

My beat also took in the fruit market, the cheese market, the fish market and bordered the meat market. Glasgow's fruit market was a lively place, abuzz with traders. It was also a haunt of crooks and scoundrels and I was always on the lookout as I strolled among the fruit sellers.

One day I noticed a young man carrying a suspicious-looking bag, which, in my experience, could have had stolen goods in it. When I caught his eye he dropped the bag and fled. I had to leave his swag bag behind as I tore off after him. It was a lengthy dash but I eventually made my catch at the fish market. But I didn't have the evidence of his crime. That was at the other market. I dragged him back there, not very confident that the stuff would still be around. I was delighted to discover that some of the decent members of society among the merchants had witnessed what had happened and had kept hold of his bag, which was filled with property from a housebreaking. Some less honest citizens would have made off with the contents but the fruit market crew were upright types who did the right thing and helped me complete the case.

Another time I nabbed a thief when I collided with a cow. I was strolling round a corner at the meat market when I was thrown into the role of a bullfighter as I saw the beast coming straight at me. OK, it was actually a side of beef that was heading my way. The chunky carcass gave me quite a clout but I recovered and realised it was being carried by a known criminal who'd pinched the slice of cow from a storehouse. There was some kind of industrial dispute at the market at the time. I'm not sure what the beef was about but it meant meat wasn't being transported from the storage premises to the butcher shops. The local 'cattle rustlers' knew there were rich pickings in there and it was a big coup to nick a big coo! I got credit for 'steaking' out the place and arresting a troublesome thief – even though it was all just a coincidence.

One day I found myself standing guard in my neatly-pressed uniform, buttons sparkling, outside the front door of Glasgow's prestigious Central Hotel. The well-heeled clientele came and went as I surveyed the scene for any signs of trouble. Quite a contrast from twenty-four hours before when I'd been trudging my Gallowgate beat as usual, seeing quite a different side of life.

It was around 1967 and I was there to provide protection for Prime Minister Harold Wilson, who was on a visit to the city. My task was to keep an eye on things at the front until the doors closed at 1am. My armed Special Branch colleagues were upstairs on patrol outside the door of the PM's room – not unusual when a dignitary of that nature was there.

Eventually I slumped into a comfortable armchair that gave me a good vantage point to watch the door. I was not spotted by two well-dressed men and a pair of glamorous young women who wandered into my earshot. It soon became apparent they weren't married couples out together. I quickly realised the businessmen were negotiating with the ladies – a pair of high-class call girls. I was quite amazed as the bargaining went on. The gents agreed on a fee of £25 for the company of both women.

I stifled a yelp of surprise when I heard the kind of money they were talking about. It certainly contrasted with the sums that changed hands among the street girls and their punters, which I knew so well. My own weekly wage at the time was £9-19s-6d, so the upmarket tarts were doing OK for themselves.

As the foursome headed off, I recalled an event that had happened just the day before. In stark contrast, I'd been working a rough area of the Gallowgate beside a down-at-heel pub. Suddenly a bloke had approached me, looking like he had something important to get off his chest. Was I going to get an earful or a crime report? Turned out he'd wanted to speak his mind. 'I'm a lorry driver and I've been all over the country,' he'd helpfully informed me. 'But this place is the lowest of the low.'

He'd gone on to explain that he'd just been approached by a prostitute who'd offered him business in the cab of his truck. Her price was a tanner! The driver had been dumbfounded that anyone could be selling themselves for such as sum – about the price of half-pint of beer or a glass of cheap vino. Although he may have been familiar with the services of hookers, he'd been mortified that a Glasgow girl would lower herself to that degree.

I'd noted his concern and the story came back to mind as I sat in the warmth of my posh hotel armchair. The call girls' £25 and the street girl's tanner were quite a wake-up call for me. In two days I'd seen the contrast between the bad part of the Gallowgate and the highfalutin types in the top hotel in Glasgow. It really

37

brought home some of the similarities and inequalities between the smart-suited and low-life individuals of Glasgow.

I was one of four bobbies in the Gallowgate and we had to deal with a number of pubs and their lively customers. At one end, the bars were frequented by the Catholic community and I was always welcomed in by them because of my surname. They assumed I was of the same religious conviction as them so I didn't tell them anything to the contrary as it made life easier. At the other pubs, which were favoured by members on the opposite side of the religious divide, I was also accepted as they knew I had all the credentials to be in the Masons if I'd wanted to.

When I was on the nightshift it was normal practice for the police to assist the publicans to clear out their watering holes at closing time, when many customers were reluctant to leave due to the effects of excessive drink. It was a good move because it meant you got to know the pub bosses and what they had heard about what was going on in the community, which was of great use to me. We usually got a free half or two when we were in but we didn't abuse the hospitality.

Out on the beat, there were regular moments of humour along with the gritty and sad side of the job. One of the bar owners preferred to stay up chatting to whoever was in there after hours, so we always left his place until last – after the sergeant and inspector had signed our books. We'd be welcomed in for a wee drink. One night I had a probationer with me when we set off for the pub about 2am. He was taking a big risk because any rookie caught smelling of drink would have been out with no questions asked.

The pub had opaque glass and the lights shone in such a way that the silhouettes of customers could be seen from outside. So we always took off our hats when we were in there because they would be very noticeable through the window.

Along with another cop, Ian, we knocked on the door and joined the lock-in. Soon we were at the bar enjoying a pint, hats removed, quite happy as everything was quiet and the bosses had headed off. Ian popped to the gents and, just then, there was a rap at the door. Three very deliberate knocks – the calling card of the polis! It could only be our inspector and sergeant! Realising the probationer was about to land in big trouble, I told him to dash to the ladies loo and hide in there. The terror-struck rookie grabbed his hat and ran to the toilets. I scooped up my hat and Ian's and dived under a large table.

Thankfully, the publican took his time unlocking the front door. By the time it creaked open I was huddled in my hiding place, trying to control my nervous breathing so I wouldn't be heard. I saw the footwear of two cops entering the pub then heard the unmistakeable tones of my superior officers. It seemed they'd had the same idea as us and they wandered to the bar to enjoy a pint, taking off their hats, of course. The quick-witted bar owner had hidden our drinks before they'd come in.

Stuck under the table, I couldn't really believe I was hiding from my bosses. It would have been comical if it hadn't been so serious. As I contemplated what would happen next, and after what seemed like ages, Ian arrived back from the toilet. He must have been stunned to see his two colleagues had metamorphosed into a sergeant and an inspector.

He was caught like a rabbit in the headlights as the inspector clocked him. I gulped as I heard the amazed senior officer say, 'Ian! What are you doing here?' It was pretty obvious but Ian was lost for words. The inspector said sternly, 'Ian, I want a word with you. I think it's best you go right now back to the police box and I will see you there in ten minutes.' Ian agreed and headed for the door. I was relieved no questions had been asked about me and the probationer and steeled myself to wait it out until the bosses left.

But things weren't that simple. Suddenly, the sergeant asked loudly, 'Ian, where's your hat?' Poor Ian didn't have a scooby that it was under the table with me! To his credit, he didn't panic.

Sizing up the situation, he said, 'Sir, with respect, I know I'm in here somewhat illegally at this time of the morning. But can I be permitted to say that you also are here illegally? Could I possibly suggest the following? When you finish your pint would you go direct to the police box and I'll appear there – with my hat.' Now I was stifling laughter over Ian's bold manoeuvre.

The two of them looked at each other and realised it was a fair point. They drained their pints and left, leaving Ian breathing a sigh of relief. He watched in surprise as I emerged from under the table, dusting myself off, and handed him his hat. He left for his appointment at the police box and I nipped into the ladies to tell the rookie cop he could come out of the cubicle he was hiding in. It looked like his career was safe. I had a keek through the window to make sure the coast was clear and we both headed off without being rumbled.

I must admit it wasn't the only time I had to hide from the gaffers. One day in Gorbals, I met up with another bobby, who took me into a local meat factory. He was a regular in there and we both enjoyed a cup of tea. But, unknown to me, the brass suspected him of malingering on the job and were on a mission to catch him dossing. When we looked out we saw an inspector and a sergeant waiting for him. They didn't spot us but we had to make our escape as soon as we could.

The two senior officers hung about for a while but never witnessed either of us exiting the place. If only they'd looked more closely at the large container lorry that drove past them soon after their arrival. Little did the gaffers know there were two cops riding in the back as it went by. We'd climbed in alongside all the carcasses before the heavy doors were slammed shut on us. A bizarre way to escape from trouble but just as well we did!

There was more alarm soon after. It was up to me to bring a violent scene to an end. In the corner of a room, a trembling man, in his twenties, was holding a knife to the throat of an older woman.

Called to a tenement flat in Schipka Pass, Gallowgate, by a distraught man who said his wife was in danger, myself and my neighbour had dashed up the stairs to find the terrifying scene we were now witnessing.

The young man, it turned out, was the woman's son. He'd been barred from the house after some sort of domestic row but had come back to cause mayhem. After kicking the door in he'd flashed a knife with an eight-inch blade at his parents. His father had managed to escape to call the police but the mother was now in mortal danger. The lad, wide-eyed with adrenalin, had his beloved mum's hair pulled back tight in his hand, leaving her throat horrifyingly vulnerable. The very sharp-looking knife was resting on her windpipe as she pleaded with him to let her go.

I was pretty new to the hostage game. On the beat in tough areas you always walked in pairs, not so much for safety, but to quickly provide corroboration of incidents, which is necessary under Scots Law. My partner was an older, more experienced cop. He was 6ft 4ins and built accordingly. A handy man to have in a fight. But this was my beat and I had to take the lead. And I was determined to ensure a peaceful outcome.

Unlike today's police, we weren't tooled up with CS spray or taser guns. We had a baton – a wee stick, really – and handcuffs. No radios to ask for back-up to rush through the door. We wore long greatcoats, not stab vests. I didn't want a scrap so my mind raced back to my training at Tulliallan Police College. What had we been told about talking down crazed people like this? Among the many things you picked up there was basic psychology. Instead of just rushing in and banjoing someone because they were up to no good, we were supposed to talk to them in a way that calmed them down.

The theory was the person would feel easier after hearing my soothing tones and come along with us to the station. Would it work? I kept asking the guy to calm down. I told him: 'This is your own mother you are threatening. You don't want to do that. Please don't harm her for the sake of an argument.' I assured him that, if he put down the knife, he could leave calmly with us. There would be no problem and nothing bad would happen to him. I tried to convince him that we were genuinely interested in his wellbeing but the situation didn't improve.

Throughout my negotiation he never spoke, just stared. It was a total stand-off and clearly at a turning point. I began to fear for his mother's safety. I tried to reason with him once again and asked if I could contact a lawyer who would oversee his safety when he dropped the knife. Again, no response.

By then we'd been there for a while and, as we had no way of getting to a telephone and were all in the living room, we couldn't call for assistance or put an ambulance on standby. The big officer who was with me had kept quiet and observed my softly, softly approach. But, as an experienced cop, he was beginning to get bored with the stand-off and my Tulliallan negotiating tactics. I assumed he wanted to rush the guy with our batons and end the whole thing in a violent encounter.

I became aware of the sound of his fingers starting to drum impatiently on the wooden sideboard he was standing next to, the repetitive pounding aggravating my already racing mind. Out of ideas and having used up all the words I could drag from my classroom play-book, I was still determined to make a final push to end it without a flashpoint. I implored, 'Look, son, I'd prefer it if you come quietly.'

At that point the drumming on the sideboard increased and my partner rose up to his full, imposing height. Fixing the lad with a steely glare, he announced, 'And I'd prefer it, son, if you didnae come quietly.' At that point the young man let go of his mother and dropped the knife. He was immediately arrested, without injury, and was eventually sent to prison. So, I learned, the psychology, although probably a good idea in some circumstances, doesn't always work.

Domestic violence is a high-profile issue these days. But in my time it was more of a hidden problem with fewer support services and a reluctance among victims to speak out. We had our own ways of dealing with wife-beaters. One man was known to go home after a night getting tanked up in the pub and inflict violence on his wife. We were called to their home many times and on at least one occasion she was so badly beaten she could have been killed.

We reckoned prevention was better than cure so we made sure we picked up the violent drunk on his way home from the pub every Friday night when he got paid. Given his volatile temperament, we could justifiably do him for being drunk and disorderly or committing a breach of the peace. He would be put in the cells to sleep it off and his wife would be spared a beating. It just became a routine that worked for everyone.

Sadly, there were many in the city who were capable of violence of an even more brutal nature, as I soon learned.

5

A WILD BEAST TAMED, THE PRINCE OF LAUGHTER AND MCLAUGHLIN'S REVENGE

As a young beat officer in Gorbals, one of the names that quickly came to my attention was Jimmy Boyle. CID officers told me to be on the lookout for the vicious crook. The locals whispered his name in fear. Boyle, still in his twenties, was a member of a gang called the Young Cumbie and had built up an awesome reputation as a hard man. Nobody in the community would speak up against him.

Born in Gorbals, his father had been involved in crime and young Jimmy had fallen into the same way of life. He'd graduated from stealing sweets and pickpocketing to more serious theft and was jailed for the first time aged 13 for breaking into vending machines. He went on to become an enforcer, collecting debts from locals who'd fallen under the spell of moneylenders.

In 1965, he was twice charged with murder but, defended by top lawyer Nicholas Fairbairn, he was cleared of the killings. However, Boyle couldn't control his lust for violence and I finally came face-to-face with him after another brutal murder.

I was at the City Mortuary in July 1967, dealing with a sudden death, when Boyle's victim was wheeled in. He was William Rooney, known as Babs, a man who had made the mistake of borrowing money from Boyle and not paying it back on time. I looked in horror at the retribution that Boyle had taken with his blade.

Rooney had been shirtless and the worse for drink when Boyle had called to teach him a lesson. After plunging a knife into his stomach, the crazed Boyle had leaned over the victim's prone body and cut his throat – the fatal wound.

The CID knew who their prime suspect was and Boyle went on the run to London where he was said to be under the protection of notorious gangster twins the Krays. But, in September 1967, as Boyle had a drink in a pub in the Smoke with fellow hoods, he was captured by undercover armed officers.

He was brought back to Glasgow, charged with the murder and put in a special observation cell at the Central Police Station. I was working the night shift and my orders were to watch the volcanic Boyle during the wee small hours. I sat on a chair in front of the bars of the holding pen – the closest thing we had to a padded cell.

Boyle's behaviour was extraordinary. He didn't sleep. Instead he paced the cell throughout the night, like a caged animal. All the while he kept his eyes fixed firmly on me. He never spoke a word and I don't think I said anything to him as I hadn't encountered him before and knew him only by reputation. I could see how he was capable of such violence and rage as he prowled like a big cat eager to pounce. It was a relief to get a break when colleagues replaced me. Boyle kept up the same intimidating behaviour with the other cops.

At his trial at the High Court in Glasgow in November that year, Boyle and co-accused William Wilson were charged with murdering Rooney by striking him on the face, body and neck with knives. A woman who was in the house at the time claimed in court it was not the pair who had committed the bloody crime. She said two men in light raincoats were behind the murder. The jury didn't believe that and Boyle was found guilty. Wilson, who had Boyle's former QC Mr Fairbairn in his corner, was cleared. Jimmy Boyle was imprisoned for life with a minimum 15-year sentence.

A number of witnesses had to receive police protection after the trial and the woman who'd seen the killing later told cops she'd been intimidated into lying about who'd done the murder. A neighbour said he, too, had been told to lie about the non-existent culprits. A second man had allegedly been forced to give Boyle an alibi. Three men were charged with conspiracy over getting the witnesses to lie at Boyle and Wilson's trial – William Wilson's brother Frank, solicitor James Latta and a hood called John Rooney (who was no relation to Babs).

All three were found guilty of approaching the female witness. Wilson and Rooney were convicted of also trying to get her neighbour to lie, while Latta and Wilson were found guilty of trying to get a man to say he'd been with Boyle in a pub at the time of the killing. Wilson got 12 years, Latta was given eight years and Rooney was jailed for four years.

The judge praised the police and the fiscal for managing to get the case to court. He pointed out that he and other judges were well aware that violent criminals had, in recent years, been acquitted because of witness intimidation and tampering and false evidence during trials.

It didn't surprise me to see that Boyle got into trouble in prison. He began a dirty protest in solitary confinement at Inverness jail and Peterhead nick and had four years added to his sentence after assaulting prison officers. Then, in 1973, he was a ringleader of a prison riot in Inverness along with three other men. One of them was Howard Wilson, a former cop who'd infamously killed two police officers in 1969. I remember seeing Wilson brought into the station after the shootings and watching one of my devastated colleagues spitting at him.

During the riot drama, a letter left by Boyle and the others was found. It indicated they'd planned to take an officer hostage and he would be killed if their escape was impeded or the media were tipped off. They claimed they'd been brutalised and de-humanised by their conditions and subjected to beatings by the guards. The relatives of their victims probably had little sympathy. Boyle was given six more years for the attempted murder of six warders.

But his life was turned around when he was transferred to Barlinnie Prison's Special Unit. Known as the Wendy House, the experiment was a secure area within the prison where the rules were more relaxed. Cons could wear their own clothes, had their own furniture and record players and were allowed their own books and uncensored mail. They were also encouraged to express themselves through art and Boyle became an accomplished sculptor and author. He wrote his autobiography, *A Sense of Freedom*, later made into a successful TV drama. In 1978, he met psychologist Sara Trevelyan, the middle-class daughter of Britain's former film censor, John, and they began an unlikely romance.

My next meeting with Boyle was around 1980, not long before his release. In the meantime, I'd had some professional dealings with at least one member of his family. But I found Boyle a dramatically changed man.

Along with colleagues from the Serious Crime Squad, I mounted an armed guard on Boyle after he temporarily got out of jail for medical reasons. He was in Glasgow Royal Infirmary for a routine operation – I think it may have been on his knees. The tooled-up cops weren't there because of any danger he posed. It was feared that the legendary hard man could be in danger from people wanting revenge against him for his brutal past.

Boyle was quite different from the prowling animal I'd watched through the night over a dozen years before. The silent, brooding criminal had become and erudite and talkative individual, who was incredibly charismatic. Ms Trevelyan was also at his bedside and I was astonished at how his attitude to life had turned around. They married in 1980 and Boyle was released two years later and became a respected artist and writer.

It was perhaps a great tribute to the Special Unit, which eventually closed in 1994. If only all the villains I encountered could have gone straight as successfully as Boyle.

It was a proud day for Scottish shipbuilding when the Queen and the Duke of Edinburgh flew to Glasgow in September 1967. Along with Princess Margaret they were visiting for a right royal occasion. The Queen was launching Cunard's new giant liner, a 58,000-ton tribute to the Clyde workers.

Number 736 from John Brown's shipyard was known as Q4 as it was the fourth ship to be named after a queen. We didn't know it until the unveiling, but it was to be called *Queen Elizabeth II*, better known these days as the *QE2*.

Before the royal party went to the Clydebank yard they had a stop-off at the Erskine Hospital for military veterans, meeting survivors of the two world wars and other conflicts. Then they were in the city centre, starting at George Square for lunch in the historic City Chambers.

It was a big deal for the City of Glasgow Police and the force wanted to put on a show for the occasion. I was delighted to be positioned at the entrance to the building as it meant the Queen would pass close by me. I'd never seen her in the flesh and I was very proud of the fact that I'd be stationed so near to her. I was really looking forward to my royal meeting but my hopes were dashed as the Queen approached.

A senior officer appeared and shouted, 'You, you and you!' I was one the 'yous'. There had already been a full security check on the building but we were ordered to carry out a last-minute search. We trooped up to the magnificent Lord Provost's Dining Room and marvelled at the sight of the long tables, elegantly set with the finest cutlery and crockery.

My job was to crawl under the tables looking for any bombs that might have been attached underneath. We gave the place the all-clear but by then the Queen had arrived in George Square and another cop had taken my prime spot. We were hurried out of the back door and by the time I got back into the square I had missed the monarch.

But I saw her later as the Queen and Prince Philip made the journey to John Brown's. A big presence of officers was required but we really didn't have enough to line the route as fully as desired. So a plan was hatched to counteract the manning problem.

In George Square I found myself lined up with other cops, looking our spick and span best, standing to attention in the style our Tulliallan training had instilled in us. I was unfortunate enough to be put next to one of the biggest bobbies on the beat – all 6ft 6ins of him. He towered over me, making me look a little less imposing in my finery. The big man's nickname was Cheyenne. He thought it came from the character Cheyenne Brodie, a heroic cowboy in a TV series from the 1950s. Little did he know we wrote it 'Shy-Ann' because he was reluctant to check back courts on his own. But no one would have said it straight to his face, if they could have climbed that high.

Cheyenne's stature always made him stand out – and this event was no exception. His head towering above the rest of the officers evidently caught the eye of one of the royal guests. As his car passed, Prince Philip did a double-take on spotting Cheyenne. Then he had another look for good measure. I spotted a smile cross his face as he went on his way.

We couldn't hang about as the plan was to move us to another location to boost the police presence. We jumped in a bus that was laid on and sped by the fastest route to the bottom of Bath Street. There we lined up again, with Cheyenne as notable as ever. The Queen's car passed soon after and the Duke had a quizzical look on his face when he spotted the stony-faced big fellow again. There are giant twins in the Glasgow polis, Prince Philip must have been thinking.

But the fun wasn't over yet. We had to jump back on the bus and proceed as fast as possible to Dumbarton Road, another location on the route. By the time his car passed a third time, Prince Philip had clocked the situation and was having a laugh at the sight of Cheyenne. I swear I could see him nudging the Queen and saying something like, 'There's that big bugger again!'

Our final stop on our bus tour was the entrance to John Brown's yard. We beat the royal party to Clydebank and lined up outside the entrance as 30,000 shipyard workers and their guests congregated inside for the most important launch Clydeside had seen since the first *Queen Elizabeth* slid down the slipway in 1938.

The royal motor rolled into sight and by now Prince Philip was ready for our unconventional 'flying squad'. He had a good look and spotted Cheyenne at his post. He was in absolute stitches as he saw the big man. Unfortunately, he wasn't introduced to us humble bobbies as, I'm sure, he would have managed one of his famous acerbic comments about the situation. But it no doubt gave him something to chuckle about as he watched the Queen cut the tape to send a champagne bottle crashing against the bow on a historic day for shipbuilding in Scotland.

Locals were amazed as I strolled down the street one day. Not by me but by the sight of my new colleague. He was a member of the Special Constabulary – the first one from the Asian community. Regular officers usually weren't too pleased to be lumbered with a Special – members of the public who wore a uniform and had full police powers. They could be nosy and interfering although some were helpful and well-meaning. Overseeing the first Asian Special was a new challenge for me.

In those unenlightened times, around 1968, some Glasgow residents didn't hide their politically-incorrect opinions. There were shouts of 'You Paki bastard!' and things were thrown at him as we walked the beat. There were no specific laws back then to deal with racist abuse and hate crimes, but the charge of breach of the peace covered a host of bad behaviour. It was always an option to 'BOP' someone, which meant doing them for a breach of the peace.

My Asian colleague, in his twenties, took some shocking abuse from the neds. But the racist ranting did at least give me the chance to lift some of the more annoying Gallowgate characters by hitting them with a BOP for shouting and bawling. Perhaps not surprisingly, the pioneering Special didn't stay long in the job.

The arrival of a Christmas card in June is unusual. In this case it spelled trouble. A woman called the office and said she'd just received a festive card from her ex-husband. The message said, 'I'm sending you this now because I won't be around at Christmas.' They'd not long broken up and she said he had shown signs of being suicidal.

I high-tailed it to his Gallowgate flat. No one answered when I knocked but I was sure I could smell gas. I booted in the door and was hit by a wave of fumes. Wet towels had been put at the bottom of the doors to let the gas build up in the kitchen, where the man was lying with his head in the oven as the fumes poured from the cooker. I had no idea if he was dead.

The whole place could go up if there was a spark, taking me and the neighbours with it, I realised. I had to act fast. Choking from the gas cloud, I switched off the cooker, grabbed the man by the ankles and dragged him through his home and out onto the landing. I managed to find a pulse. Fortunately, I'd recently been to a first-aid course and I knew what to do. I pumped his chest as I fought to resuscitate him. Eventually he began to choke back to consciousness and I alerted my ambulance colleagues before heading back into the flat to throw open the windows and let the deadly fumes disperse. I was awarded a Commendation for my lifesaving exploits although I have no idea what happened to the suicidal man.

Interestingly, people were often arrested for breach of the peace for attempting to take their lives because it allowed them to be taken into custody and have their mental health assessed.

Another suicide bid later led to a startling situation on a busy street near Hampden Park while I was in the CID at Gorbals. Driving past with my colleague, I saw a naked woman rushing along the pavement in broad daylight, blood dripping from her head and over her body. It looked like a scene from a horror film. Had she been attacked? We pulled to a halt and got hold of her, covering her up before taking her to her home nearby. As we waited for medical help, she explained as best she could what had happened.

She'd decided to hang herself from the pulley over her bath. She'd stripped off – don't ask me why – and stood on the edge of the bath as she'd looped the rope over the pulley and round her neck. But the pulley had given way under her weight and she'd fallen and cracked her head on the edge of the bath, eventually coming round to find blood pouring from the wound. Semi-conscious and confused in her bloody condition, she'd rushed into the street, hardly aware she was nude. Fortunately, her naked ambition to end her life had failed.

Like the Military Tattoo that is a feature of the Edinburgh Festival, there was a City of Glasgow Police Tattoo in 1968, showing off the skills of the force's pipers, horses, dogs and parading officers. I was among those who took part. The organisers needed guys who could march so they looked for those with military experience. My time in the Boys Brigade stood me in good stead for the event, which raised cash for the Stars Organisation for Spastics Scotland.

The extravaganza was at the Kelvin Hall and I remember one of the funniest moments came when a senior police officer had to preside over the General Salute. Nerves got the better of him and he got his words twisted, announcing to the assembled company, 'Seneral Galute.' He must have felt like a galoot after that!

Two years later I got caught up in an international police tattoo in Glasgow. But I wasn't taking part in this Kelvin Hall extravaganza, which included bands and a police motorcycle display from Italy. My role came on the Saturday night at the end of the week-long event when the bandsmen retired to a city centre bar to relax. There wasn't much entertainment on offer in town after about 10pm in those days and the mood in the pub began to become stale. It was obvious that, far from home, the musicians were yearning for female company. It was made known to me and my colleagues that our task was to help out the lonely visitors, who'd come from across Scotland as well as England, France, Denmark and Holland among other nations.

Attempts to get hold of enough female police officers and nurses from the Royal Infirmary and elsewhere proved almost fruitless. So we set our sights on ladies who were more readily available. We jumped in a van and toured the red light district, scooping up all the street girls. They were given a clear choice. They could go to jail or they could head for the bar, where they would probably have a good time and get plenty of drinks bought for them. It was obvious which option they'd go for.

The ladies of the night were delivered to the scene of the carousing and the pipers and drummers were none the wiser, believing some charming Glasgow gals who'd been out on the town had turned up to greet the visitors. We didn't say too much about where they came from and we knew the women wouldn't be daft enough to try and charge the bandsmen for their company. Had they tried that, they'd probably have ended up in the pokey the next day. I remember one of the dolly birds made a beeline for a big bandsman, reckoning the unusual job was better than the regular routine on the streets. What went on later between the girls and the tourists, I can only guess at.

It was quite a scene, with cops and a few senior members of the legal profession enjoying a yahoo. But there was a hiccup when the rocking venue was raided by our police colleagues over after-hours drinking. The inspector who was on the case probably hadn't been put in the picture about what was going on. With all those legal minds at hand, his warrant was studied and a 'mistake' in it was spotted. Would he mind rectifying it and returning in an hour's time, he was asked. He obliged and, when he returned, everything was found to be in order.

At that time, one particular family were known for creating absolute hell around the area. They'd been forced out of the previous place they'd lived in by local vigilantes. When they landed on my patch they were known for lobbing things out of windows at officers checking back courts, committing thefts and being responsible for anti-social behaviour on a grand scale. They were such a nuisance that everybody wanted to see them get their comeuppance in the hope they could get rid of them.

The parents had the weans well trained. If you went looking for one of the kids at their home, none would admit to having the name of the one you were seeking. Even the youngest of the clan, aged about three, knew not to identify any of her siblings to the cops.

At one point the 14-year-old son went on the run from an approved school – a residential institution where young people were sent by the court. One day I spotted him from a nearby police box, leaning out of the top-floor window of his home, painting his name on the wall so everyone could read it. That's one way to keep a low profile! We had to go into the house 'four up' – with four officers – as we knew we wouldn't be welcome. I arrested him and he went berserk, punching me in the face and kicking my partner.

I was to be the star witness at his trial and I couldn't wait. I got information that a number of members of his troublesome family would be in court. Some were to be defence witnesses, others were planning to watch the proceedings.

Seeing an opportunity, I went to the records office to look up the family members due in court. First, the father. He had an outstanding warrant. Next, the brother. He had a warrant, too, albeit for a minor offence. The sister was in the wanted club too. To top it off, two of the lad's cousins were turning up. I didn't want to miss out his extended family so I checked them out and hit gold. Another two warrants needing enforced.

The only member of the clan I'd be seeing that day who wasn't wanted was the mother. She was a real mean matriarch, who protected her brood ferociously and was always uncooperative when we turned up to investigate their criminal activities. But her nose was clean this time.

So I went to the court and gave my evidence, despite the evil looks I was getting from the hard-faced mother and her family. Success! The boy was found guilty and the stipendiary magistrate told him he was going away. At that point there was a stir in the court. I'd positioned colleagues from my shift in the public benches and they were advancing, warrants in hand.

Each pair approached a member of the crime clan and informed them they were nicked. I'd had to get ten cops to go to the trial unpaid to ensure the result we wanted and it was a measure of the upset the family created within the area they were all delighted to volunteer to help me get them locked up.

I hadn't warned the court or the fiscal that I was planning the creative move so there was much scratching of heads among the lawyers and rumblings of discontent from the ambushed crooks. But they were bang to rights and were led away to the cells soon after the lad had been taken down.

But the seething mammy was disgusted that I'd trapped her mob and got them the pokey. Realising I was the mastermind behind the sting operation, because I'd been the key witness against her son, she spun round and stared at me with fury. Spitting pure venom, she shrieked, 'McLaughlin's a f***ing bastard!' Ach well, it was water off a duck's back to me.

But my delight was complete when two court officers stepped forward and immediately arrested her. She was being done for contempt of court. Not because of insulting me though. The magistrate happened to be called McLauchlan. In the eyes of the court staff, she'd called the judge a bastard and that just wasn't on.

As she was led off, it was amusing to note that we'd got her even though she was the only one without a warrant. The fiscal was so taken with the course of events he mentioned it to me every time I saw him after that. It was a satisfying six-out-of-six in my battle against the family from hell, who eventually moved out of the area to the delight of the locals. However, folk in their new residence didn't like them any better and soon got up a petition to have them moved. They were off my patch but I had sympathy for anyone who had to deal with them.

6

THE FACE OF BIBLE JOHN, THE SORRY HEID AND A ROYAL SURPRISE

The name Bible John sends a chill through the folk of Glasgow and Scotland as a whole. The notorious slayings of three women in the city in the late 1960s horrified the nation. But the murders of Patricia Docker, Helen Puttock and Jemima McDonald remain unsolved.

I was a beat bobby in Bible John's hunting ground during the panic, when every man in town was eyed suspiciously to see if they matched the photofit of the killer or the memorable artist's impression showing what he was supposed to look like.

In late 1969, I spotted a bloke who had a striking resemblance to the wanted man. The encounter, which came after the third murder, was near the Barrowland Ballroom where Bible John picked up his victims. I was on the lookout for anyone fitting the description and I noticed a suspicious character near the ballroom eyeing up passing women. He then tried to swap coats with another man – a ploy used to attempt to fool the bouncers if you'd already been refused entry.

I sauntered up to him and was amazed by his dramatic reaction. He turned on his heels and sprinted along the street! After a chase I cornered him in a dead-end alley. But he picked up a brick and threw it at me. It missed and, as he stooped to grab another brick, I drew my baton and struck him with it –

the first of only two occasions I had to use it throughout my career.

He was hauled down to the police station where he admitted his first name was indeed John. A colleague and I took him to the Royal Infirmary for a medical check. The young doctor insisted the prisoner's handcuffs should be removed – despite my warnings that our man was violent.

The doctor was determined to be in charge and ordered us to stand outside while he looked at his poor patient. Free of his cuffs, the suspect attacked the doc. We heard a commotion and the shattering of glass and rushed back in. My prize catch had escaped – by throwing himself through a closed window. The treatment room was on the first floor and he'd plunged to the ground before making off through the car park and into the night.

Of course, we knew who he was so I filed a report stressing that he should be looked at by the Bible John inquiry. CID men tracked him down and I believe he was ruled out because he didn't have the distinctive overlapping front teeth that were said to be a trait of the killer. But I felt he was a pretty good suspect at the time.

It's ironic that I nabbed the man over his resemblance to the painting because I've never been convinced it was an accurate portrait of Bible John. I met a witness who stared into the face of the murderer – and continually insisted the artist's impression was nothing like the man he saw.

He worked at the Barrowland and was the senior member of the security staff. He'd encountered Bible John during an incident before the killer had left the dance hall with the last victim, Helen Puttock, and her sister. The man who became the most mysterious figure in Scottish criminal history had caused a fuss when a coin that Helen's sister had put into a cigarette machine had got jammed.

The steward, who I believe has since died, was called to tackle the situation. He got a very good look at the man and had a clear recognition of the event. That trick of folk changing clothes with their pals to sneak back in meant the big security man had to have a keen eye for faces. But when he saw the Bible John painting he insisted it was wrong. He wasn't even sure about the killer's trademark red hair!

Given his job, I saw him as a credible witness. I met him many times and he never budged from his opinion. But the investigation team put more store in other witnesses and I wasn't going to make a fuss about it because I was a young officer trying to get on in the job.

The portrait has become one of the best-known and most haunting images in the annals of crime. It was painted by Lennox Paterson, of Glasgow School of Art, and released by police seven weeks after the murder of Helen Puttock. Hundreds of men fell under suspicion because they resembled the likeness of the red-headed, fine-featured suspect.

The artist's impression was painted with the help of Helen Puttock's sister, Jeannie, who always insisted it was accurate. She'd spent time in the company of Bible John at the Barrowland and during a taxi ride. He was given his infamous nickname because she revealed he had made references to the Bible, although it's thought what she said about his religious utterances was probably exaggerated by others.

I'm certainly not suggesting she deliberately misled the detectives and I'm sure she would have been convinced of her recollections. But it's no secret that Jeannie, who passed away in 2010, had enjoyed a wee drink on that fateful night although she always insisted she hadn't been more than tipsy. It's notoriously difficult for eyewitnesses to remember things accurately. I once worked on a case involving a robbery victim who insisted the suspect was 5ft 4in. When we caught him he turned out to be 6ft 2in.

It begs the question – could the cops have been chasing a phantom? Was the real Bible John able to go about under a cloak of anonymity because the face being hunted was wrong and would never be found?

My brush with Bible John didn't end there though. Nearly 25 years later I was running the force's Criminal Intelligence section and had the chance to review the Bible John files through the eyes of modern policing. All unsolved crime files were under the control of the Criminal Intelligence Department. It was fascinating to read the official details of the legendary and gruesome killings, which many cops believe weren't necessarily carried out by the same man.

I noted with interest that semen had been found on the clothing of Helen Puttock. That led me to write a report for top brass, suggesting that they should employ the burgeoning science of DNA – genetic fingerprinting. If they could get a DNA profile from the body fluid, there was a strong chance that whoever it matched was the killer. I filed my comments and moved on, thinking no more about it.

But DNA was eventually used in the hunt for Bible John in 1996. There was an ambitious, yet fruitless, attempt to tie one prime suspect to the crime. He was John McInnes, who'd faced four identity parades at the time of the crimes. But when his body was exhumed in an expensive operation he couldn't be linked to the DNA profile the police had developed.

It emerged in 2004 that detectives had been DNA-testing suspects from the time of the three killings in a fresh bid to solve the mystery. At that point I brought my fears about the accuracy of the iconic artist's impression to the attention of Strathclyde Police. But they didn't want to know, saying they were happy the image of the killer was based on information given to the senior officer at the time by key witnesses.

In recent years there's been suspicion that Scottish serial killer Peter Tobin was the beast behind the murders. Photos of him as a young man are said to resemble the artist's impression – if that means anything, given what I've said above. But he's too short in stature and DNA hasn't fingered him. And so the Bible John mystery lives on.

One of my regular 'haunts' on duty was a Gallowgate pub with a spooky reputation. The Saracen Head is a Glasgow landmark. The original inn, built in 1755, was on a site across the road from the bar's current location. Patrolling the area on dark nights in the late '60s, I would easily have agreed with local legend that the pub was haunted.

There were certainly some spooky noises that came from the building as I wandered the darkness outside. To add to the scary atmosphere, the pub was home to the skull of Maggie, said to be the last witch burned at the stake in Scotland. Maggie's head is still in the Saracen Head, on a shelf next to some tankards.

These days, the ghost of a former owner, Angus Ross, is said to inhabit the pub. Angus was a fixture behind the bar in my heyday and his family owned the pub for a century. If the stories are to be believed, Big Angus is still keeping an eye on the building in spirit form.

I had many dealings with Angus at the Saracen Head, or the Sarry Heid as it's known in tribute to the sorry, sore heads that follow a night of carousing in the tavern. Angus gave me a guided tour of the place, which was something of a museum, with guns from Jacobite times and a handwritten poem by Robert Burns on the wall.

The original inn was a terminus for the stagecoach from London and had stables for 60 horses in the 18th century. It was regarded as one of the finest hotels around, advertising that all its beds were free from bugs. Angus told me about the large fireplace in the original pub where Dr Samuel Johnson and his companion James Boswell sat and relaxed when they returned from their tour of the Hebrides in 1773. He pointed out the grate, which was from the original fireplace, where they had tapped their pipes.

Angus once gave me a call to ask what would happen if he handed over a head that had come into his possession. Would there be any questions? It sounded intriguing. Was I about to get involved in a brutal murder involving decapitation? I hot-footed it to the Sarry Heid and found Angus with a twinkle in his eye.

He produced a poly bag from under the bar and handed it to me. Sure enough, it looked like it contained something shaped like a head and fairly heavy. When I opened it I realised I'd been had. To my relief, I wasn't looking at a real human head. It was part of a statue that had been vandalised. I was grateful to Angus as I'd been on the hunt for the sculpture's heid for a few days.

The statue stood in a fountain at the rear of the Saracen Head buildings where musical events were sometimes staged. It had evidently had its block knocked off by crooks looking for scrap metal. They'd taken the head off to check what the statue was made of and had evidently decided it wasn't worth lifting the whole sculpture to sell for scrap. How it came into Angus's possession, I didn't know and I didn't ask.

It was in the Saracen Head one evening that I had a hair-raising experience – quite literally. We were surprised when the owner Angus called the police for help dealing with a troublesome customer. Big Angus was well over six feet tall and usually had no problem handling rowdy or violent drinkers. But something about this guy had really alarmed him.

There must be serious trouble kicking off, I thought, as I headed into the pub. The air of tension among the customers was clear and I could immediately hear a man shouting and bawling about something. He had his back to me and when I approached him and made my presence known, he spun round and eyed me angrily. His face was contorted with rage – but that wasn't what left me open-mouthed.

To my amazement, his hair was standing on end! Not because he'd given himself a spiky look with Brylcreem. Whatever combination of anger and other emotions he was feeling had made his hair stand up straight. I'd never seen anything like it and neither had Angus the publican or his staff. No wonder they'd called for back-up to deal with the crazed man. I've no idea what the enraged customer had become so worked up about, although too much drink was probably involved.

Before I could grab him, the snarling man made his move. Luckily, he didn't attack. He turned on his heel and burst out of the bar. It looked like I was in for a foot race. I dashed after him as the customers looked on in confusion, no doubt relieved to see the violent drinker call last orders on his remarkable floor-show.

Our sprint from the Gallowgate continued towards Glasgow Cross. Along the way I tried to halt his progress by chucking a number of my bits of equipment at him. I wasn't trying to injure him, just impede his progress. I hurled my torch, which missed. I didn't have time to stop and pick it up. Later I had a go at throwing my baton at his legs in a bid to slow him up with a sharp surge of pain. My aim was off again but at least I got my stick back as I wouldn't have wanted it falling into the wrong hands.

As I continued to yell at him to give it up, I was thinking about lobbing my handcuffs in his direction – anything to stop the hot pursuit. But he was pumped full of adrenalin and seemed to have tapped into a super-human strength to carry him forward, even though he was boozed up and hadn't had my gruelling fitness training.

I'd seen this phenomenon before. When folk were fleeing the police they could be driven by an unusual force which gave them the ability to perform unlikely physical feats. I remember chasing a guy into a back court and assuming I had him cornered. But I watched in disbelief as he ran up a 12-foot wall and jumped over it to escape. It's very hard to catch crooks when fear puts wings on their heels.

Whether my hairy prey was driven by anger or fear, he took some catching. By the time I grabbed him at Glasgow Cross and charged him with breach of the peace, we were both shattered and whatever quirk of biology had made his hair stand on end had subsided. His hair had flopped back down and he was too tired to battle me. Apparently, the term for hair standing on end due to the fight or flight mechanism of the body is called 'piloerection'. Whether that accounts for an angry man with hair standing straight up, I have no idea. I've seen it only once – and that was enough.

In the car one day, I was racing to a call and determined to get there as fast as possible. I put the lights and siren on to clear a path through the traffic. Around Glasgow Cross a motor in front tried to pull to the side to let me past but the driver came to a quick halt rather than slowing at a reasonable rate. There was sickening screech of my brakes as I tried to avoid the obstacle but I felt a thud and heard a crunch as I clipped the back of the car.

After hopping out to check that the driver wasn't injured, I established there was no major damage to either car. I went on my way to the incident, annoyed but not unduly worried. But my accident came at an inopportune time. There happened to be public disquiet about police cars going too fast through the streets and some people were calling for a clampdown.

That week, it seemed, a number of cops had got involved in some sort of prang. Either minor like mine or a bit more serious. And can you believe it? We all got charged with motoring offences. Not anything heavy like reckless and dangerous driving but a lesser charge – careless and inconsiderate driving. I was determined to fight this slur on my skills behind the wheel as I felt I had done my best to avoid the accident while going at a reasonable speed given my mission to get to a crime scene quickly.

A knowledgeable member of the traffic department gave me a good tip. He asked if the car didn't stop as quickly as it might have when I put my brakes on. If so, he said, I could claim a 'latent defect'. What's that, I wondered. He said that, in a percentage of cars on infrequent occasions, the brakes didn't work properly when the pedal was pressed. It was reasonable for me to say it didn't slow down. A latent defect wouldn't be obvious in a check on the car by a mechanic as it didn't show up often. But once in a blue moon it would crop up again.

'How can anyone disprove a latent defect?' I asked.

'They can't,' smiled the wise old owl.

When his traffic cop colleagues came to charge me they apologised as they did the deed. I replied that I believed a latent defect had affected the braking system. They were surprised and impressed to hear me using the term.

I pled not guilty and ended up in court. My lawyer told me to sit tight as he wouldn't be calling me to ask any questions. One key piece of advice he gave during the hearing was to uncross my legs – apparently the sheriff didn't like that casual look.

But the man on the bench was known as a big supporter of the boys in blue and, looking at his face, I deduced he reckoned the whole case was preposterous. I imagined he saw me as a young guy who'd been putting his life in danger driving quickly to a scene to tackle crime. The fact that the prang hadn't resulted in injuries or write-offs meant the whole thing was a farce, in my opinion.

But I was still expecting a court battle as the witness, the car driver, began to give evidence. The driver verified his details and the date of the accident. He described how the cop car had clipped the back of his vehicle and confirmed I'd had my lights on and he'd realised I was behind him. 'I tried to get out of the road but I might have been a wee bit slow,' he admitted. This was going better than I expected.

Then he was asked, 'Do you see the driver of the police car in court?' It was pretty obvious who that was. But he replied, 'No, I don't.' That was a bonus. It looked like he was as unenthusiastic about the prosecution as I was. 'I'm surprised we're in court,' the driver continued. 'That guy was only doing his job.'

My lawyer turned round to the sheriff and proposed that the case should be dropped through a lack of identification. Of course, a check on the police records would have confirmed that I'd been the driver. But there was no stomach for the ridiculous situation to go on any longer.

There was no need for me to use my latent defect defence. In the quiet court room, with just me and the lawyers, the sheriff announced, 'Case dismissed,' then gave me a sly wink. Punishing cops for going about their job obviously wasn't on his agenda.

In 1969, I began working in plainclothes. If you were a bobby who was interested in getting into CID, that was the way to go to impress on the bosses that you had the right stuff to become a detective. I did a year in that role.

Princess Margaret was on a visit to Glasgow and there had been some sort of threat to her safety. She was staying at the city's landmark Central Hotel, several storeys up. So anyone trying to get at her would have to either go through the front door or climb up a rone pipe outside and get to her room that way. Our job was to make sure that nobody was hanging around or had broken in. With my partner, I took up residence in the splendour of a room opposite the royal guest's suite to ensure we could keep our eyes and ears peeled for trouble.

After the princess had headed off for a gala evening in the city, the Lord Provost's assistant suddenly appeared at our door with a round of drinks on behalf of his prestigious boss. 'Just to say thanks for your sterling work, lads,' he explained as he left us our tipples.

So much for the old adage about not drinking on duty. It would have been impolite to have turned our noses up at a snifter from such a high heid yin. We gurgled back a few glasses as we kept guard.

Then another fellow appeared with a further tray of drinks. This time it was from the hotel's head of security, who wanted to show his appreciation too. It was down the hatch again with a couple more liveners. By this time, it's fair to say, we were a bit tipsy. Perhaps not the best state of affairs when on royal duty. Hopefully there would be no hiccups to come!

But as we continued our watch, we heard a distinct noise from the direction of Princess Margaret's bedroom. Could the thudding sound be trouble brewing? We stealthily, and a little unsteadily, made our way to the door and, having permission to go in, turned the key and entered. Fortunately, it appeared that all was quiet and that no-one had broken in.

I was struck by the opulence of the room and spotted a collection of posh glossy magazines, such as *Horse & Hound*, laid out for the royal guest. But the most eye-catching sight was a large china sculpture of a swan on a silver tray.

Admiring the bird, I gently touched it. Disaster struck. It wasn't made of china at all. What I'd taken for ceramic was white icing. The swan was a fancy cake! My fumbling fingers knocked its neck squint and smudged its eyes. What a sight! We were looking at the ugly duckling's mother.

So the two bobbies attempted as best we could to fix the problem, delicately using butter knives to smooth out the smudged eyes and gently trying to realign the crooked neck without knocking the bird's head off. We didn't do very well and we beat a hasty retreat, fearing there would be a scream of horror from inside the room when the princess returned and spotted the state of the damaged gateau. That would be big trouble for us.

The princess came back in later, true to form, bouncing off the walls after a good night out. We heard no more about the cake incident so I assume she and her entourage didn't spot the cross-eyed swan when she tottered back into her suite. Then again, maybe she thought she'd knocked it squint herself or perhaps the pastry chef got blamed for a botched job.

Drugs weren't such a pervasive problem in the late '60s. So it was something of a novelty when I heard one of the local pubs was allegedly awash with illegal substances. A big drugs bust would go down well so an officer went in undercover for a snoop around and confirmed that pills were changing hands. We didn't know if they were LSD tabs or some other type of illicit substance.

We launched a full investigation, even setting up cameras in a building opposite the bar to monitor proceedings. We spotted one guy hanging about outside the pub for long periods. Turned out he was selling tabs for a pound a time. He told his customers it was great stuff but he warned them not to take it until late in the evening for the best effect.

He was grabbed by us and his pockets were full of the mystery tablets. But when we took them back the station for a closer look our big drug swoop turned out to be a bust. The pills were Swizzels fizzy sweets. They were individually wrapped in foil to make them look convincing but their only kick was a sherbet rush.

The conned customers who had been drinking away and yahooing had no idea they were getting no real effect from their 'pills'. The fact that they had been advised to pop them late in the evening, when they were drunk, helped maintain the pretence.

The dealer was making a fortune from the drugs mugs so I suppose he was guilty of fraud in some way. But essentially all he'd been doing was selling sweets so we got nothing from our major operation. However, his trade was ended and no doubt his clients would have had a stern word with him after learning he'd been selling them sweets in his Swizzels swizz.

I got a name for being good at nabbing pickpockets. Proactive policing was key. It was vital to get information about when the light-fingered crooks would be on the move. I once got a tip that a gang was set to get a bus into town to target the crowds at the Pavilion Theatre. They would hit as the audience coming out of the first sitting of the show merged with the crowd going to the second sitting. It was easy pickings for them and wholesale slaughter among the thronging theatre-goers.

But, thanks to our operation, we hoovered up eight of them in a single swoop – something of a record. One of the young lads had a fiver in his possession that led us to solve another theft. A woman had been walking along Argyle Street and had opened her pay-packet, which had a number of brand new £5 notes in sequential order. Just then, a ned had passed by and grabbed one of the fivers out of the middle with a polite 'thank you'. We knew the serial number of the money and it turned out our pickpocket was responsible. We certainly cashed in on our theatre crack-down.

In 1970 I was involved in a raid on a lively premises – a shebeen. They were illegal drinking dens in houses and were quite common. This one was right in heart of the Barras. It was Sunday when we burst in with our warrant and found the locals enjoying their illicit booze.

We all had our jobs to do. Some officers had to nab the house-holder, who was running the place. Others had to grab a handful of customers who would be witnesses. My task was to collect up all the bottles of booze and the optics. It was mission accomplished fairly quickly but there was a development we hadn't expected.

This was a shebeen with in-house entertainment provided. On top of a large table in the centre of the living-room stood a stripper. She had a skimpy garment on her lower half and nothing but a pair of tassels on her top half! A record player in the corner had been providing a musical accompaniment to her gyrations before our rude interruption.

We hadn't been expecting that. What's more, we weren't sure what to do with her. She wasn't drinking and she wasn't an organiser of the party. So we took her details, thinking she'd maybe make a witness. She revealed she'd been working in London as a good-time girl and also honing her stripping skills in Soho. She'd recently returned to Glasgow and was now caught up in a situation that was getting her worried.

'I can't go to jail,' she pleaded, unaware she wasn't likely to. 'Is there anything I can do?' One of my colleagues obviously couldn't resist having some fun and asked, 'What is it you do with those tassels?' Showing a remarkable knowledge of the subject, he added, 'Is it true you can make one go round one way and, at the same time, make the other one go round the other way?'

She agreed it was a talent she possessed and he fired up the record player so she could give him a successful demonstration. The rest of us tried to avert our eyes and get on with our duties, thinking it wasn't every day a sight like that was served up at the Barras.

7

BECOMING A DETECTIVE, AN EFFECTIVE INFORMANT AND THE WRONG MEN

Getting into the CID was a tough task in my day. It seems that in the modern force officers are just told they're to become a detective and can sometimes spend a short time in CID. The start of my 27-year career as a detective wasn't so easy. You had to have a minimum of four years' service before applying and at least have your sergeant's ticket, in other words, have passed the sergeant's exam, which you could only sit after four years.

For a while I was a CID 'aide', which meant I learned about everything the department had to deal with but I didn't formally hold the position of detective. It was their way of finding out if you were the guy for them.

In 1971, there were around 23 people from across Glasgow Police battling for one vacancy as a detective in the Central, the most sought-after division in the force. It had everything except a prison and a football ground, including the police HQ, the Scottish Criminal Record Office, the High Court and the Sheriff Court, all in centre of Glasgow. Then there were the lively surroundings of the Gallowgate, Townhead and Gorbals.

The list was whittled down to four and I was delighted I was one of them. The job not only meant a greater challenge but more money. There was a detective's allowance, a clothing allowance and another extra payment. You could make the same as a uniformed inspector and the regular hours of the job were 8am-6pm.

I was put through a gruelling interview by senior officers, including the detective chief superintendent of the CID and the detective chief inspector at the division. I felt I did well and my experience at solving crime, especially pickpocketing, while in plainclothes and as an aide, stood me in good stead. I knew two of the other cops who were up for the job but the third was a guy who was well-connected within the force and I feared nepotism might help him land it. We all anxiously waited to hear who would become a detective constable the following Monday.

By the end of the week I had heard nothing and my spirits plummeted. I called the other two guys I knew. Neither of them had received any word. Well that was it then. I'd missed out and the remaining applicant, with his good contacts, must have succeeded. I left on Friday feeling low but, in the way of the police, it wasn't as simple as that.

On Sunday I got an early call from a DC at the Central. 'You've got to be in here by 10am,' he announced. 'You're going to London.' I was perplexed and asked him what was going on. 'You're the new detective we're expecting,' he revealed. Looked like I'd been promoted after all – and I was starting a day early! I hardly had time to absorb the good news as I threw on my suit and headed to the office before the flight to the capital to pick up a criminal and bring him back. When I returned the uniformed divisional commander saw me and waved his recognition. He'd forgotten to tell me about my promotion. That was typical of the way things worked.

My first murder case as a detective was a stomach-churning crime scene in the Townhead area. Lying on a bed was the battered and bloodied body of an elderly woman. Her maggot-infested remains were a horrific sight.

It was pretty obvious early on who the prime suspect was. The victim's granddaughter was in the frame. The officer in charge thought the old woman had been killed with a brick because her head was caved in. His suspicions were raised because there were bricks lying at the entrance to the close and it looked like she may have brick dust on her wounds.

But it was a good thing the girl was charged with killing granny with 'a brick or similar instrument'. Always best to cover all the options in these cases because it wasn't a brick at all. When the body was finally moved we found the murder weapon under her pillow – a big hammer.

After the scenes of crime officers had done their bit, lifting prints and photographing the victim, we had to think about preserving the bed and bedding as evidence. The body was taken away but we wanted to halt the march of the maggots from the bed and kill them off. After all, we'd probably have to search the place again for clues and we didn't want the bugs to get all over the room in case we got a paw-full of them when we were sticking our hands into nooks and crannies while we were looking for any evidence.

The trick we used was to sprinkle a chemical in a circle around the bed. That kept the maggots from moving out of their location and hopefully killed them off too. A cop was left at the door and we returned a couple of days later to a more manageable and less distasteful scene.

I got caught out by the new-fangled airport metal detectors when I flew down to London to pick up an armed crook, who had been caught for us by the Metropolitan Police. I arrived and took custody of the man, who had been found with two handguns in his possession. We called the airline to alert them that we'd be bringing a prisoner onto a flight and the usual arrangements were made. He was given a window seat to keep him secure and we had a discreet spot on the plane so we could slap handcuffs on him unnoticed if he became difficult at any point.

Marching through the security check at the airport, all hell broke loose. As I unknowingly wandered through the metal detector, not realising what it was, all sorts of bells and whistles sounded. Soon I was surrounded by anxious security staff. They all went white as sheets when I casually explained the problem: 'It must be the guns I've got in my coat,' I smiled. They all took a flaky at the mention of firearms.

Before they could grapple me to the ground, I managed to pull my police warrant card from my pocket and explain I was entitled to be carrying the weapons. I asked to speak to the airport police and we had a quiet word in their office as I filled them in on my mission.

The flight crew were alerted to the need to carry firearms along with the felon and the captain had an unusual demand. He insisted that the guns had to ride with him in the cockpit. We had no choice so we took our flight and the criminal gave us no problems. We were last off the flight and went to the cockpit to ask, 'Please sir, can we have our guns back?' After that experience, I was well aware of metal detectors at airports.

Now I was a fully-fledged CID man, based at Cranstonhill Police Office, and faced my first nightshift in charge. The nightshift guy covered the whole of the division, so I had to have my wits about me. When I got a call to action from the uniformed inspector, I jumped to attention. He was like a god to us, controlling the whole shift and the sergeants. There was a death, he reported.

I raced to the scene where the inspector was waiting. 'There you go, son,' he smiled, handing it over to me and disappearing. I had to swallow hard as I realised this was it. I was in charge and having to make the decisions. I could have rummaged about other divisions to get some help but it was time to stand on my own two feet.

I studied the picture. A woman was lying dead in bed, her clothing disturbed. Her top half was exposed, her underwear removed. She was probably only in her thirties. Surely not a natural death? Could it be murder? I noted a couple of glasses. It looked like she'd had a visitor who was drinking with her but he'd obviously scarpered.

I swept into action. The glasses were collected to check for fingerprints. The police photographer captured the scene. I noted there was no sign of forced entry to the city centre flat. The neighbours reported that they hadn't heard any arguing or raised voices. Family members told me the dead woman was someone who enjoyed going for a bucket at the local boozer, often picking up a new fella along the way – nothing more notable than that. The relatives gave me the name of a possible boyfriend but I had no address for him and couldn't get any further with that info at the time.

But by then I was doubtful it was a murder. Something in particular began to convince me that this probably was not foul play. I'd stared at the faces of murder victims before and had often seen the pure terror etched on them. But this woman was different. She had half a smile playing across her face. There was nothing disturbing about the scene. I reckoned she'd died having sex. The exertion combined with the booze had done for her, I believed.

I headed back to the office to write up a full report for the detective inspector to read when he clocked on in the morning. I outlined my theory that it was a natural death, adding prosaically that I thought she had 'died in ecstasy'. Perhaps not the most polis-like language but it seemed to sum up the situation and her Mona Lisa smile.

Feeling I'd done everything to the best of my ability, considering it was the first time, I clocked off and went home to bed. But my slumbers were shattered by a call around 8am. It was my DI and he wasn't happy. He shouted and bawled at me about the way I had handled the woman's death and demanded that I get myself into the office straight away. I suspected he was annoyed he had missed out on an overtime payment because I hadn't called him out during the night.

I told him she had died of natural causes, probably through intercourse and all the drink she'd had. 'I wouldn't classify it as a murder,' I insisted.

'You don't know that,' he sniffed, continuing to berate me.

I asked, 'Have you had a post-mortem?' still confident that it was a sudden death.

'We'll have the results in a few hours,' he barked.

'Call me back then, I'm going back to sleep,' I said.

Of course I never got that phone call and when I went back on duty that night I made a point of checking what the post-mortem had revealed. Yes, she'd died of a heart attack.

We tracked down the guy she'd been with and he backed it up. He'd panicked when he'd realised there was something seriously wrong with her and had just run out of the door. It was an interesting incident in my study of the detective's trade. Here was me, taking full responsibility and making difficult decisions and all I got was a lot of hassle for my trouble.

Just the next night I got mixed up in another memorable case. I got a call from the divisional control room telling me that a publican I knew from the Gallowgate wanted me to contact him immediately. It turned out that he had another pub in the Cranstonhill area, my current patch.

He gave me a car make and registration number and told me where it was parked. He said I'd get a nice surprise if I searched the boot. His staff had overheard two men and two women talking that night about having to dispose of certain items that were in the boot. My informants didn't know what the dodgy gear was or the names of the four characters involved. They weren't regulars in the boozer but the two men gave the impression of being gangsters.

With the help of fellow detectives, I staked out the car. It wasn't long before the two men and their girlfriends staggered towards the vehicle. By then we'd checked it out and knew it was a hire car. We pounced as they climbed into it and asked if we could have a look in the boot. The driver obligingly handed over the key. I was surprised he was so helpful until I took a closer look at what I had. It was just the ignition key. There was a separate key for the boot and it was missing. Frustratingly, there was no way into the boot through the back seat.

The driver, of course, claimed he was never given a boot key from the hire company. By now drink had overtaken them and they were no longer playing ball, no doubt realising we were on to them. As they grumbled, they and the car were taken to Cranstonhill where they were detained. Before the days of micro-chip car security systems, getting into a motor wasn't so difficult. We had a selection of spare car keys at the office. After a bit of fiddling, we unlocked the boot and opened it up like a gang of eager treasure-seekers looking inside a pirate chest.

There sure was some booty in the boot! We found two sawn-off shotguns, a handgun, two masks, ropes, naval uniforms, several thousand in pound notes and a large quantity of drugs. One major armed robbery, which had taken place earlier that day, was solved on the spot. The other stuff we recovered included property stolen from a merchant ship berthed on the Clyde.

The men were, in the records of the Criminal Intelligence Department, classified as Main Index offenders – career crim-inals. They were convicted at the High Court in Glasgow of the robbery and the other related crime. The women were prostitutes who frequented the ships where they plied their trade and pinched the uniforms, which were used as disguises by the men during the robbery.

A phone call from an informant proved how a tip-off can be worth its weight in gold and can save the police a lot of time and money in major crime investigations. After my earlier row with my detective inspector, he had to admit he was pleased with that particular result.

Coincidence often played a part in my job. It helped me out once when I went for a haircut. We'd had an alert from the police in Berkshire that a man was wanted over a major incident. A police officer had been murdered – shot in the head after stopping the man and his associate in a stolen car. The notice said the fugitive had friends in Glasgow and might turn up in the city.

Eager to crack the high-profile case, I looked up the man's details. I was interested to see there was another crook with the same unusual name. He was a big-time conman and, as I read his file, I realised he was more likely to be on my patch than the first guy. I memorised the details of both criminals just in case they appeared on my radar.

I took a break to pop across the road to the barber's. As I sat in the queue waiting my turn, my attention was drawn to a big guy getting a trim in the chair. I looked at his face in the mirror and was stunned. He was the spit of the conman I'd been reading about earlier. He fitted the description at well over six feet tall and had some other distinguishing features. So I decided to offer the barber shop customer 'something for the weekend' – in this case a police cell! After slyly creeping out of the shop I asked a colleague to join me and we grabbed him when he left. It turned out it was definitely him. He was wanted in a number of countries on warrant and his details had been circulated by Interpol, so he was a big fish to hook. Newly-coiffed and reeking of aftershave, he was the type you wouldn't buy a used car from. But he was obviously good at his conning ways.

I'm fascinated by the way criminals work and what makes them tick so I had a long chat with him even though it wasn't my case. He was quite open with me, confessing he'd let his family down with his devious lifestyle. He'd been to Israel and other countries, running up bills at posh hotels by using a false name. He would help himself to as much food and booze as he could before doing a runner.

He was a master of using fake documents to assume a false identity, which he inhabited with skill, convincing people he was that person and defrauding them. He told me he'd first realised the potential of misusing official paperwork when he'd noticed his grandfather's date of birth was only one digit different from his own. Grandpa had the same name as him so a delicate touch of a pen and a change of photo ID provided him with a passport without having to apply for one. Misusing the document to get up to no good had been one of his early exploits. I was enthralled by his brass neck. I have no idea what his punishment was as I was only the arresting officer and didn't follow the case through.

I reckoned it was always worth seeing a crook face-to-face, even if you didn't have an immediate reason to speak to them. One of my habits in CID was to check out the major criminals in person at their homes. With a colleague, I'd knock on their door and, after getting some abuse on introducing myself, would ask what they wanted. They would be confused and I'd say they'd called me out. They'd deny it – because they hadn't. It was just my ruse to see the criminals in the flesh so I could recognise them about town in the future. I'd insist someone had called the station from their address and they'd tell me to get lost. Then I'd head off, happy I'd achieved my aim.

An informant contacted me with some juicy information about a robbery in the south of Scotland. He identified a man who'd carried out the theft after hiring a car with a fake driving licence. He gave me the man's full name and description, including hair colour, age and where he was from. He also told me where the hire car had been dumped after the raid.

It looked like he was right on the money when I went to the spot and found the car. I had it recovered and checked forensically. As often happened, the driver had adjusted the rear-view mirror, leaving a lovely thumb print for us. I sent it off to the fingerprint experts to see whether it matched my suspect.

I then headed to the Scottish Criminal Record Office to find out more about my target. He had unusual first and second names. So I flicked through the card system and quickly found him. He matched the age – in his twenties – and the description, and was from the right area. He had a lengthy record that put him right in the frame for the kind of robbery I was investigating.

The fingerprint came back. It wasn't his but that wasn't crucial. Someone else could have left it in the rental car. I was happy that my tout had given me good info and I arrested the suspect. He was quizzed and vehemently protested his innocence. But I had three witnesses – staff from the car hire place. They all positively picked him out at an identification parade. So I had my tout's information and good eyewitness evidence. I confidently charged him and sent my report to the fiscal.

Satisfied with another job well done, I went about my business. But not long after I found myself in the middle of nightmare scenario surrounding the case. I bumped into my informant and asked him if he had anything for me. 'I'm giving you nothing,' he grumped. 'You never did anything about the last name I gave you.' I protested that I'd picked the guy up but he was insistent he'd seen the suspect strolling the streets without a care in the world. I tried to humour my tout as I wanted to keep him sweet. Had I heard the name wrong? No, it was right.

I told him to leave it with me and I went to look into it. By then that unmatched print was preying on my mind. Back at the SCRO I looked through the card index again. I found my man and flipped from his card to the next one. My stomach turned over as a wave of anxiety hit me. There was a second man who had exactly the same unusual name! He was the same age, had the same hair colour and was from the same area as my man. The coincidence was even more incredible because they weren't related! What were the chances of two people with identical information – criminal doppelgangers?

I decided to do a discreet check with the fingerprint bureau. They confirmed the thumbprint matched the second man. The realisation that I'd arrested the wrong person left me reeling. I agonised about what to do. But then I had a stroke of luck that got me out of jail – and would keep the wronged 'twin' out of prison. I heard that two of my three witnesses had emigrated to Australia and wouldn't be available to give evidence at a trial.

I let the fiscal know that the case was severely weakened because of that and, much to my relief, he marked the file 'no proceedings'.

The man had a high-profile lawyer but he accepted it all and never complained. I had cause to rebuke myself though. It was a frightening situation that could have led to a miscarriage of justice. With three witnesses and an informant lined up against him, the guy could have been banged up for a stretch. I had never come across anything like it and it was a hard lesson for me that something that seems black and white may not be so clear cut.

In another case, a garage was raided and block-and-tackle lifting equipment stolen. A neighbour gave us a description of a vehicle, including the make and colour and a partial licence number. It sounded like one owned by a well-known crook who targeted garages.

When I arrived at his home I stumbled upon an Aladdin's cave of stolen goods. I couldn't move for cardboard boxes, stacked high. Many of them were stuffed with expensive knitwear from a company in the Borders. There were other items, such as handbags and accessories, in the cartons. We needed two police vans, crammed to bursting, to take away the booty from the home in Dennistoun. The block-and-tackle wasn't among the stuff we recovered.

The criminal was furious to be losing the valuable haul and was convinced I'd been tipped off that he had the gear. He told me he knew who my informant was and he was going to take revenge on the 'grass'. I advised him not to, informing him no one had given me any information. But the crook wouldn't be convinced.

We proceeded with a cracking case but shortly after that it took a bad turn. A man was found badly injured in the East End. His legs had been broken, his nose smashed and he'd been slashed with a blade. He told cops he didn't know who'd attacked him but he was sure of who'd sent them – the man we'd found with the knitwear. It looked like, as promised, he had taken his brutal revenge – on an innocent man.

I went back to him and told him he'd made a mistake but he didn't believe a word I said, perhaps not surprisingly. Turned out the injured man was involved in the thefts. He worked at a railway depot where the goods had been stolen and had delivered them to the crook. We couldn't get the bad boy for arranging the beating but he was done for reset. I was just sorry that a man was given a doing because we'd solved a robbery by luck.

The impact of a police investigation can make a dramatic difference to the twists and turns of a life. There were even times I felt I was indirectly responsible for someone's death. Around 1973, I was on the hunt for a suspect over the fraudulent use of cheques. I turned up at his door and his partner told me he wasn't around. She eventually admitted he was in a local pub so I set off to pick him up. But when I arrived, I'd just missed him. The barman said my man had received a call before he'd left. Presumably the girlfriend had tipped him off that I was on my way.

What happened next turned a routine inquiry into a tragedy. The suspect had hopped in his car and made off. But a police traffic car ended up behind him. It was just a coincidence. The officers didn't know he was wanted. But the suspect thought the cops were on his tail and he panicked.

As he drove through the Southside, he put his foot down and sped away from the police motor. Now he had their attention. They realised that a car suddenly haring off meant the driver had something to hide so they put on their siren and raced after him. A high-speed chase followed and the two vehicles roared along streets and screeched round corners. However, the fleeing criminal didn't have the driving expertise of the cops, who were fast catching up.

In a desperate bid to escape he put his foot to the floor but lost control of the motor. The man, who was in his twenties, wrapped the car around a telegraph pole and was killed instantly. The cop car coincidence meant he got a death sentence for trying to elude my investigation into a fairly minor crime that would have only earned him a fine.

Another time, ten years later, when I was in the Serious Crime Squad, I got a tip about drugs. A young man who had a reputation as a user was holding a load of cannabis, my informant told me. At his home, a well-kept flat in a multi-storey, the suspect, in his early twenties, was nowhere to be seen. But the lad's father invited me in. He was not happy to see me but allowed us to search the place. His disgruntlement was evident and he voiced the opinion that we were unfairly picking on his son, who was clean of drugs by then, he claimed. I told him I was working on good information that there was a quantity of dope on the premises.

But could we find it? Not a chance. Every room was gone through in a specific manner. Once a space had been searched, a bobby stood by the door to ensure nothing could be concealed in there afterwards. It began to look like the father's annoyance was justified. As he gave me an 'I told you so' grimace, I thanked him for his cooperation and left with my colleagues.

Not long after, the father called me, his voice quiet and his tone humble. 'I wanted to apologise to you,' he explained. 'You were right. My boy was still mixed up with the drugs when you came round.' Then he stunned me by revealing, 'He's just died from an overdose.' I gave him my condolences. He was a decent man who, I imagined, had done his best for his son through his substance abuse problems.

I have to say that after hearing that news it niggled at me that I hadn't managed to find the boy's stash. That way I could have lifted him and he may have got some help from the justice system rather than sinking further into the mire of drugs. But what could I have done? I'd been through that flat from top to bottom.

When I later encountered the informant who'd given me the tip on the cannabis, I asked him if he had any good information for me. 'You didn't do very well with the last one. Why didn't you arrest him?' he said dismissively. When I told him the supposed drug stash had not materialised, he revealed something that made my heart sink. 'You didn't look in his car, did you? The stuff was in there.'

I hadn't even considered the possibility of a car and his dad hadn't mentioned one. If I'd been visiting a house I would doubtless have passed by the car and taken it into account. But being at a multi-storey, I hadn't associated the resident with a vehicle. I was left kicking myself. Firstly, for failing to find the gear but secondly over the possibility that a successful drugs recovery could have prevented the young man's death.

In both these cases I was probably being too hard on myself, thinking I could have done something to prevent the tragedies. I couldn't be responsible for the welfare of people who had taken a wrong turn in life. But it was something that occupied my mind at the time and that I still think about now.

8

THE RED-EYED ELEPHANT, THE CON ARTIST AND THE AWOL CONFESSOR

When I walked into the businessman's office, I was taken aback. I'm not normally lost for words, having seen a catalogue of incredible sights in my time. But I hadn't expected to stroll into the heart of Africa in Glasgow's Brown Street.

It was the early 1970s, and, in an office designed to look like a Zulu den, Maurice Cochrane sat at his desk. The cheeky Cockney, who preferred to be called Big Jim, had an outlandish backdrop of animal skins, rifles and spears on his wall. For good measure, he was wearing a traditional safari suit, topped with a pith helmet. I wondered if he was taking the pith out of me – or was just barking mad.

Toupee-wearing managing director Big Jim was pleased to show me around the factory, Rotary Tools, which he had opened in the mid-1960s. In his office, as a huge circular fan rumbled above our heads, he invited me to have a coffee while he pointed out his bizarre interior decor. Among the unlikeliest of the features was a large toy elephant, big enough to sit on. Big Jim told me he forced job applicants to clamber onto the blue tusker while he interviewed them. He warned them that Ellie, as he called it, was a lie detector.

Big Jim, in his late forties, chuckled as he asked me to look at the elephant's eyes. They suddenly lit up red. 'That's how Ellie indicates that you're lying,' he laughed. Maybe the police could do with an elephant like that! He showed me the concealed wire that ran from the elephant to a button under his desk.

Another of his furry friends, which I didn't encounter, was a teddy bear. It was the company's personnel manager. He'd sit with the ted as another ruse to catch folk off their guard. Big Jim reckoned it was a way to size up super-smooth salesmen. What better way to catch them off guard than to have a toy bear ask them cheeky questions like some kind of twisted ventriloquist's dummy.

If they got the job, the salesmen were made to perform a ritual when their figures weren't adding up. They were forced to kneel in front of a Chinese idol called Bung-Ho and ask for inspiration in dealing with their customers. It turned out the 'bung' in the idol's name was significant. Its teachings included whether to slip a client a bottle of whisky or treat him to a slap-up feed to grease the wheels of industry. An exercise bike also sat in the corner. The boss would often cycle, wearing very few clothes, during meetings.

Big Jim was obviously one of those types who tried to impress people. He certainly made an impression on me although probably not in the way he hoped. He perhaps saw himself as a paragon of the business community but to me and my colleagues he was a colourful character who needed to be watched.

He'd come to our attention as someone who had a criminal past. In the 1950s he'd been jailed for a few months at Glasgow Sheriff Court for stealing a van full of carpets. Later, in the south of England, he'd been banged up for four years for burglary and thefts. We realised he had an adventurous past and his future could become troublesome and cause difficulties on our patch. He regularly called the cops to complain about business problems – threats from rivals, that sort of thing. But he was never keen to lay out the full details when we visited. I suppose he was just putting down a marker in case of future problems, warning people he'd let the police know something was going on.

It was decided that a small number of officers should deal with him so we could get to know what was going on. I was among those who made several trips to Rotary Tools to hear his gripes. He was always entertaining and tried to ingratiate himself further with the cops by inviting us to a lavish party in August 1973. He promised it was to be the must-attend event of the year with over 2,000 'close friends' enjoying free food, booze and a live performance by legendary jazzman Dizzy Gillespie. I gave it a body-swerve as did most of my colleagues. We didn't want to be caught in the crossfire if things went bad for Big Jim, as we feared they eventually would.

But, being cops, we kept our ears to the ground to find out who was there and what happened. Not that it was much of a secret, given the way the do progressed. In the end over 4000 folk turned up. Dizzy and his band, who'd been flown in from the Continent, could hardly get to the stage to take advantage of the £3,000 lighting set. Musician Humphrey Lyttelton had also been booked but pulled out and was replaced by Ray Ellington. Folk couldn't get near the bar for the free booze, which included 4,000 bottles of spirits, Jim later claimed.

There was a belly-dancer and the new Miss United Kingdom chose the occasion to make her first public appearance since winning the title. Ambulances stood by and cops were on duty.

At one point people queued along nearby Carrick Street into Argyle Street. It was just as well Big Jim had gone to the trouble of knocking down a factory wall to make extra space for a marquee to be erected. He'd to fork out to put the wall back up again next day as I doubt he had planning permission for the remodelling job.

After the tunes from Dizzy's trumpet, a pipe band took over, marching down Brown Street at 5am. The musicians were paid about £4,000, taxis home for guests cost £300. The hostesses were usually paid £10 a night for pouring drinks and entertaining. The flamboyant businessman later boasted that the party, which was to mark the opening of new premises, cost £47,000. The new building cost only £26,000.

There were plenty of big-shots among the guests including one, our intelligence told us, who would go on to become one of Scotland's most senior politicians. Not that there was any suggestion any of them were doing anything untoward at the party. Big Jim was just a generous businessman at the time. But his lavish use of money was to get him into trouble not long after.

He ended up in court in 1976, accused of bribing business contacts and providing women for sex. A disgruntled former employee, who believed he was owed money by Rotary Tools, blew the lid off the shenanigans at the factory.

Big Jim and a colleague faced sixteen charges covering the period 1969 to 1974. The charges, under the Prevention of Corruption Act, included fraud, attempted fraud and providing the services of women in return for favours. They were accused of supplying glamorous girls to businessmen at a Glasgow hotel and of giving money and gifts to officials in major Scottish firms and engineering companies in England. Big Jim was also charged with defrauding firms down south to the tune of £12,500. In a bizarre accusation, befitting of his unusual ways, Jim was also said to have fixed a beauty contest so his secretary could win it. Carolyn Schulz, who later became his wife, scooped the Miss Airpower 1973 title, and Jim was accused of convincing the judges to vote for her. The unlikely charge was later dropped along with three others.

But there were claims he had proposed to Carolyn to ensure that, as his wife, she could refuse to give evidence against him. But she denied that and claimed she had been attracted to him because of his flamboyant, forceful nature. However, she revealed he was an emotional mess and on tranquillisers. He even had to go to the loo at set times, which caused problems on flights because he couldn't bring himself to use aeroplane toilets.

Down on his luck as the trial approached, he took to standing in the open air, shouting, 'Knickers!' No, he hadn't finally cracked. He was reduced to helping Carolyn sell ladies underwear at Ingliston market, near Edinburgh.

Other officers had prepared the case against him but I, like the enthralled public, followed the antics outlined during the trial. The five-week court case was described as one of the longest and most bizarre in Scottish legal history. A string of red-faced businessmen were quizzed about taking cash and gifts, or consorting with girls who had been laid on to smooth the business deals.

One of the star characters was a Polish model called Anna Lanska. Although, for the purposes of her court appearance, she reverted to her real name – Anna Grunt. It turned out to be an appropriate surname, given the role she played. The 25-year-old strawberry blonde was a leading photographic model on the books of a top Glasgow agency. She explained she'd been a hostess at Rotary parties along with other girls from the agency. She'd been approached by a staff member, on behalf of Big Jim, and was made an indecent proposal. Would she sleep with a client for cash?

Miss Grunt said she had agreed to do so for £35. She claimed she'd slept with a second businessman for the same amount. Big Jim later revealed his famous teddy was called Grunty in tribute to his Polish glamour girl. He said he felt bad about her being dragged into the trial as it had damaged her modelling and acting career, which, he claimed, had included working with famous director Roman Polanski and, ironically, playing a virgin in a Monty Python movie. Another woman, an ex-Bunny Girl, also admitted going with a Rotary Tools client at a Glasgow hotel.

Well-known lawyer Ross Harper represented Big Jim and said he wasn't guilty of corruption, just a victim of extortion by clients who had a variety of tastes. Mr Harper told the court, 'One man's meat is Anna Grunt, another man's meat is tickets to boxing matches and another man's meat is cash.' He added that his client was a big spender who would have delighted songstress Eartha Kitt with his generous ways.

While his co-accused was found not guilty, Big Jim couldn't talk his way out of this one. The jury took six hours to find him guilty of eight charges. Interestingly, on three of those he was convicted of, the jury added riders that he had paid out money under conditions and threats. Businessmen had made it clear they wouldn't do business without a payment. As for the role of Anna Grunt, he was found guilty of providing her services to a client. By then 51, he was jailed for 12 months as the judge told him, 'This is not a court of morals.'

After his conviction more details emerged about the eccentric boss's behaviour. Starting work in the afternoon, he'd expected his salesmen to hang around until he left in the early hours. Many of them ended up on tranquillisers, it was said, due to the relentless schedule. There were tales of blue movies being screened at Rotary parties and women and pornography being used to aid business deals. Cheeky salesmen would pose as clients to take advantage of the girls. One was caught and made to write out a cheque to cover his unwarranted freebie.

Big Jim was said to have ruled by fear, humiliating sales staff at meetings and firing people on the spot. At one point, it was claimed, he held a mock trial with a young staff member as the accused. Others took on the role of prosecutor and defence counsel as the man had a spotlight shone in his face. He was, naturally, found guilty and sacked the next day.

He'd tried his hand at acting as a young man, so Big Jim put on some dramatic performances for potential employees, bursting in during interviews and berating the colleague who was talking to the applicant. There would be fencing matches using the ornamental swords on the walls, which drove away stunned job-seekers.

When some staff left he allegedly tried to undermine their business by getting people to parade outside their opening party wearing sandwich boards. They carried religious messages, as did the leaflets handed to startled guests.

When he got out of jail, after serving eight months, Jim had lost a few stone but was still as gallus as ever. He cropped up in a confessional in the papers, boasting of his previous crazy life-style, saying he'd only behaved that way because he felt that was how a tough businessman should carry on. The one-time £10,000-a-year boss claimed that bungs were a part of business culture and he had done nothing worse than many others, including some of the most upright members of Glasgow society.

It was no surprise to me and my colleagues that Big Jim came a cropper. We had spotted the potential for trouble as soon as he hit our radar and we knew he could be heading for a fall. How right we were.

He was a likeable rogue, which is how I'd describe most of the con artists I encountered. Often they were very clever. They had to be to undertake their scheming. Rarely, if ever, were they violent.

One of the most intriguing was Sammy Cowden, a time-served conman with a well-honed modus operandi, or MO. I first came across him in 1974 when I was a detective constable in Cranston-hill Police Office. I was called to the home of an elderly lady, who told me she'd been the victim of a cunning fraud. Although I didn't know it then, the culprit was Sammy.

Several days before, he'd knocked on her door and said he'd made a special journey to visit her. She'd listened as Sammy, a plausible character in his forties, explained he'd just arrived in Glasgow from Sydney, Australia. He'd introduced himself using a false name and said that Down Under he'd run into one of her relatives, who lived in Australia. She did have family in Australia so she was interested to hear more.

Sammy said he'd been entrusted with delivering a package to her – all the way from Oz. It must be from her nephew, Billy, the woman thought, and mentioned the name. Yes, it was from Billy,

Sammy confirmed. He'd never met any of her relatives but he was delighted to seize on the name she had offered him to make his story more plausible. He was invited inside and they had a nice blether over tea and scones. All the while, Sammy used his blagger's skills to pick up information that would be useful to him. His host asked how Billy was getting on. 'Does he still have black hair or has it turned grey like the rest of the family?' she enquired. She let slip so much information about her relative that Sammy didn't bat an eye when she looked out the family photo album.

He'd heard so much about Billy that he could easily pick him out in the pictures his victim proudly showed off. His highly developed conman's craft left her in no doubt that he had met her nephew and he easily ingratiated himself with her.

When she asked excitedly where Billy's parcel was, he moved into the second stage of his operation. His tale was that he'd left it in his hotel, which was in Edinburgh. He hadn't wanted to carry the heavy package all the way to Glasgow in case he couldn't track her down.

That's not all he'd left in the capital, he revealed. His wallet was still in his hotel room too. It was full of Australian notes but he'd used up his only British money – a fiver – travelling through to trace her, as he'd felt duty bound to do. It was the weekend so he couldn't get more British pounds until the bank opened on Monday.

Just as Sammy hoped, the kind-hearted pensioner went to her purse and handed over a £10 note to get him through the weekend. Cleverly, Sammy had not asked her for any money. She'd offered it assuming the friendly visitor from Down Under would return with the parcel and her tenner. Of course, she never saw him again.

Suspecting the grifter was using a well-worn routine, I called at the City of Glasgow Police headquarters in St Andrew's Street to speak to Len Bisset, who worked at the Scottish Criminal

Record Office, which was established in April 1960. He was an expert at identifying suspects from their Method Index file, which contained the MO of known and suspected criminals. He quickly gave me Sammy's name.

Sure enough, his victim picked out a photo of him. Turned out Sammy had been done for the same thing many times before. His rap sheet was so long he was invariably sentenced to jail time after pleading guilty when he was caught.

He liked to pick on vulnerable, elderly ladies. How did he find them? He'd examine the brass nameplates beside tenement doors and look for sparkling ones. Those with names that had faded through years of proud polishing usually belonged to older ladies. After finding his way into the close he'd knock the door to see if his hunch was correct. He gambled on the fact that women of that generation usually had a relative in Australia. Sometimes he'd claim to have come from Canada, which was another sound bet.

Since he hadn't asked for money, no crime would have been committed if he'd used his own name rather than a false one. That meant he'd committed a fraud. I didn't have the pleasure of meeting and arresting Sammy that time. Another officer nabbed him and he pled guilty, meaning I didn't see him.

But my dealings with Sammy weren't over. He came back on to my radar in 1987 when I was a detective sergeant in Gorbals. By that time he was 61, but he hadn't retired. As usual he had conned his way into a lady's home, calling himself John Maxwell on this occasion. But he had to use all his years of experience to charm himself out of what looked like a situation where he could be rumbled. Over tea and biscuits, he was doling out his usual patter when his target's two sons suddenly arrived along with one of her nephews.

Sammy was outnumbered and facing male adversaries, which didn't follow his blueprint. They were suspicious of him but he pulled out all the stops to convince them he'd run into their cousin Archie in Sydney. They were delighted to hear Archie was doing well and pleased that he'd sent them a parcel.

As usual, Sammy put the bite on to extract some cash. He gave them some story about having problems using his travellers' cheques and was given £30 by one of the sons. Sammy said his hotel was near Byres Road, and he'd head there to collect mum's parcel later.

But the lads took a shine to 'Mr Maxwell' and decided to take him out for a drink first. Sammy followed them to the local social club, where the family was celebrating a birthday, and the carousing began. But, much to Sammy's alarm, he became involved in a round of drinks. He wasn't willing to give up any of the £30 in his pocket so he made for the exit before it was his turn to go to the bar.

Another family member spoke to him as he left and Sammy couldn't resist one more con. He gave a sob story about not having enough money for a taxi and extracted £10 from the Good Samaritan. Relieved, Sammy made it into the street to hail a cab.

He climbed into the taxi, confident another day's conning had succeeded, when two of the lads he'd met earlier jumped in beside him. They reckoned they'd share a lift into town with him since they knew he was going to his hotel near Byres Road. Sammy had to think fast again but he was up to the task. He exclaimed that he'd just spotted an old pal on the street and asked the taxi driver to pull over. He thanked the boys for their hospitality and said he'd see them later, before disappearing into the night. Of course, he hadn't paid his taxi fare.

Again he'd made the mistake of using a fake name so I was on his tail as soon as the family reported the crime. After my first brush with Sammy, I knew who I was after. A trawl of the local homeless hostels located him the next day. Ironically, he'd signed in using his real name instead of a false one, which made him an easy catch.

Not unusually, he pled guilty and was jailed. He told me he didn't mind being sent to prison because it meant he knew where his next meal was coming from. Sammy spent a lot of time in jail for what was not exactly the crime of the century. No violence was ever used by him and the victims handed over money rather than having it stolen behind their back.

When he was caught he accepted his actions and took the punishment. I spent an hour talking with him in the police cell and was left in little doubt that he was almost the consummate fraudster and would have been more successful if he had forgotten about his obsession with the Sydney con.

He was like an old uncle and appeared to be very genuine. It didn't surprise me that folk invited him in and were happy to make him 'one of the family'. There was nothing intimidating about him, as far as I was concerned, and he was charming rather than despicable, like some con artists could be.

Although he was homeless and lived in the models, he didn't look like a tramp. He was well enough groomed and had a certain standard of dress that didn't arouse suspicion. The modellers, as the residents were called, were generally clean and respectable, people who'd fallen on hard times and needed a place before getting on the ladder to get housing and a fresh foothold in society.

Sammy was clever in the way he committed fraud by implying what money he needed and letting his victims hand it over. But he had no great strategy. He just struck when he could, where he could. He was a true opportunist.

In 1998, about a year after I retired, Sammy was in the news headlines. Cops throughout Scotland had launched a crackdown on con artists, named Operation Hamelin. Sammy was caught in their trap and dubbed 'King Rat' by the officers. He was 72 by then but that hadn't stopped him spinning his web of lies in Glasgow, Clydebank and Edinburgh. His Australia tale hadn't passed its sell-by date and he'd hit at least 12 victims, the oldest

87, who'd handed over amounts up to £140. At the time he was on the run after going AWOL while out on licence from his latest spell of porridge. He was jailed for six years, seemingly incapable of giving up his life of conning.

I was met with a touching scene when I went to investigate a housebreaking in the mid-1970s. The homes were luxurious tenements in the Woodlands area and I was welcomed into the flat by an elderly lady, who must have been in her eighties.

She showed me some of her home then ushered me into the living room. There I saw a unique sight – a large apple tree. It was in a huge pot and the unusual item of interior decoration had obviously been growing for many years. Its branches spread up a wall and across the ceiling. It was an astonishing sight and I had as many questions about the tree as the robbery.

Speaking quietly, tears in her eyes, the pensioner told me the tree was a tribute to her late fiancé, who'd been killed in the First World War. Before he'd left for battle, he'd given her a gift of an apple, which I think was quite common then. She'd kept it and, on hearing the shattering news of his death, had planted the seeds. Over the years she'd propagated it into a sturdy tree. I was astounded by the moving tribute to lost love. She'd obviously never married after the wartime tragedy sixty years before.

'It wisnae me, guv!' It's a plaintive cry I was used to hearing from suspects, even those who were bang to rights. A confession was always a bonus. But there was one admission of guilt it would have been better to never have heard.

The bizarre series of events made an entry into my collection of legal firsts. It began in October 1975 when the Royal Bank of Scotland in Argyle Street was raided. A lone gunman pointed his weapon at the terrified cashier and ordered her to hand over the money. He got away with nearly £2,500 but, fortunately, no one was injured.

As a DC at Turnbull Street's Central Division head office, I was handling the case. There were few leads and I wasn't getting very far. Then, two weeks after the robbery, I had an unlikely call. It was the Military Police. It was always nice to hear from my Ministry of Defence counterparts, especially if they had some useful information for me. They were calling from the Army Training Centre at Pirbright in Surrey. They told me one of their Scots Guards had admitted to the bank robbery in Glasgow, where he'd been absent without leave since September until the local cops had nabbed him and handed him over to the army.

While being transferred to the base he'd spilled his guts to the MPs and had shown them a newspaper cutting detailing my case. Better still, he'd taken them to where he'd hidden, at the army base, a gun he claimed he'd used in the raid.

I headed down there with my colleague and we interrogated the soldier – 21-year-old John Boyle, from Glasgow's Easterhouse. He offered a detailed confession in a voluntary statement, which he signed. Back in Glasgow, I arranged an ID parade so the traumatised teller could pick out our man. She didn't identify him. Puzzlingly, she didn't even look twice at our self-confessed bank robber. She was insistent the man whose gun barrel she'd stared down wasn't in the line-up.

My doubts began to kick in. After all, Boyle's confession could be described as circumstantial at best. Then I clocked her hair. He had claimed in his statement she was blonde. But she confirmed she had black hair at the time. She assured me it had been the same colour on the day of the robbery. I looked closer at the press cutting that had been in Boyle's possession. It wrongly reported the cashier was blonde. Had he picked that up from reading about the robbery rather than first-hand knowledge?

My concerns grew more when I showed the witness the gun Boyle claimed he'd used to hold her up. No way, she said. The weapon she faced was a black one with a small barrel. Boyle's was an old grey one with a long barrel. And how did he manage to hide it at the army base if he'd been in Glasgow for a while?

My heart sank further and I began to mull over the case again. I hadn't managed to recover any of the stolen cash from Boyle. He'd hardly had time to spend it all and he had none in his bank. He hadn't given any of it to his friends and relatives. There were no new threads on his back – his clothes were old and tatty.

Boyle's explanation was a strange one. He'd handed over his ill-gotten gains to the IRA, he said. His unusual tale began in a pub in Glasgow. He claimed he'd been approached by a man who'd noticed he was in uniform. The stranger asked if he'd served in troubled Northern Ireland, which he had. On finding out Boyle was Catholic, the man had urged the soldier to leave the army and use his skills to rob a bank! Boyle claimed he did as suggested and then gave all the money to the terrorists.

The combination of the unlikely story and the teller's evidence gave me and my colleague real concerns. However, we decided it was best to put forward the case as it stood, complete with his admission, and let the procurator fiscal decide how to proceed. After all, it was hardly likely an innocent man would confess to such a major crime.

He freely admitted the robbery to his lawyer and pled guilty by submitting a Section 102 letter to the court. That was a letter from his solicitor to say he was pleading guilty, meaning there was no need for a trial. He was sentenced in November 1975. When he heard his punishment – nine years – Boyle suddenly did a dramatic U-turn. He protested that he was innocent! It looked like my fears were coming true.

Boyle then made another confession – that he was guilty of being an idiot. He'd only admitted the crime to avoid being sent for punishment in army prison – the dreaded glasshouse. Turned out Boyle had discussed contrasting conditions in military and civilian jails with his escort, an army sergeant, while he was being taken south from Glasgow. On hearing about the tough conditions in military clink, he'd begun to ponder his options. He didn't like the sound of army jail and had opted for Barlinnie instead in the hope of an easier ride.

He'd reckoned a spell in civilian jail would be preferable to six months or a year in the glasshouse for going absent without leave. He hadn't expected such a long sentence, thinking he'd only get two years.

He was given an appeal – and what a strange one it was. The judges said the circumstances were 'extraordinary if not unique' as Boyle now claimed he was 'wholly innocent'. What's more, the prosecutor agreed! The judges opined, 'The learned Solicitor General made it clear that investigation has now demonstrated that there was never in fact any evidence available to the Crown that could corroborate the applicant's admission of guilt or his circumstantial confession.'

They added, 'In this unique case, there can be no room for doubt that there has been a miscarriage of justice.' But Boyle wasn't getting off scot-free. The judgment continued, 'For the predicament in which he finds himself, the applicant must bear a heavy responsibility for his deliberate, detailed and repeated false admissions and confessions.'

Boyle had his sentence quashed but, in April 1976, was given six months for attempting to pervert the course of justice. He was immediately released due to time served. But the army promised he wouldn't escape their punishment and that he'd be returned to them for his case of being AWOL to be considered. I'm not sure if he got shut in the glasshouse after that but the army did admit to the press that Boyle was correct in his belief that their prison was tougher. 'More intensified discipline' was how they put it.

I was perfectly entitled to arrest him given his confession and I was content when we proceeded with the case. It was our man's crazy behaviour that caused the problem and the concept of a false confession hadn't been on my mind when I was dealing with him. Our action wasn't criticised in the appeal judgment. So, from a police perspective, I was happy with the way it was dealt with, bizarre though the case undoubtedly was.

9

AN UNSOLVED ATTACK (OR IS IT?) AND AN ANIMAL ID PARADE

When a man called Peter Tobin was convicted in 2007 of the murder of a young woman in Glasgow, it sent a shiver down my spine and sent me searching through my files for an old photofit of a sex monster I hunted but never caught.

Tobin, then 60, killed Polish girl Angelika Kluk in 2006 when he was working as a handyman in a church, using the fake name Pat McLaughlin. He beat, raped and stabbed her before dumping her body in a void underneath the church floor. Tobin was convicted of her murder in May 2007. His background, including attacks on two young girls, made me wonder if he could be the car park rapist I'd investigated in 1975. It was the first time I'd been the lead detective on such a serious case so I remembered well the details and the frustration of not getting my man.

I saw Tobin on TV after the Angelika Kluk trial, assaulting a photographer as he was led from the court to a prison van. I immediately thought, 'If he is the right height, he is my man.' I'd kept the photofit of the knife-wielding attacker and it seemed to me it was chillingly similar to photos of a younger Tobin in the newspaper coverage of the Angelika Kluk case.

Reports said Tobin was being probed over a string of murders and rapes, including the disappearance of Scots schoolgirl Vicky Hamilton in 1991. He was later found guilty of killing her and burying her in his garden. He also concealed the body of another young woman, Dinah McNicol, in the garden of his house in Margate in Kent.

The 1975 attack on a 24-year-old woman in a Glasgow multi-storey car park happened on a Saturday evening in December. The victim had said her attacker was aged 25-29. Tobin was 29 at the time. The glove-wearing rapist was around 5ft 7in. Tobin is 5ft 6in. He had brown hair and a local accent – like Angelika's killer.

I scoured the newspapers for links between Tobin and the 1970s sex attacker. The rapist wore a jacket, shirt and tie. Tobin was said to have preferred to dress in a suit and tie rather than casual clothes. The attacker had a moustache. There were reports that Tobin had a habit of growing one to change his appearance.

And the Glasgow rapist had threatened the woman with a knife – one of Tobin's trademarks. He'd repeatedly stabbed Angelika and had been convicted of attacking two teenage girls in 1993, raping one of them after threatening her with a kitchen knife. One of his ex-wives said he'd stabbed her with a knife he'd always carried and another claimed he'd flashed a blade at her.

I felt the man I'd hunted was probably someone who'd moved around. Tobin was living in Brighton in the mid-1970s but was known to return to his home patch to see his mother in Renfrew-shire. Could it be that he was behind the horrific crime decades before?

The victim was getting into her car on the second floor of the Waterloo Street car park at around 5.30pm when the attacker threatened her with a knife and made her kneel on the floor on the passenger side while he drove to the lonely sixth floor. There he stole cash from her handbag. But this was no robbery. It was a serious sexual assault.

I gave Strathclyde Police a copy of the photofit and a report of the crime from the *Police Gazette*. They couldn't say anything officially about any unsolved crimes linked to him but I took comfort from knowing that insiders close to the team investigating the fiend said they were aware of the car park rape and others possibly linked to Tobin. However, they cautioned that getting proof after all those years was the problem. Whether the evidence had been kept, I have no idea.

Strathclyde Police ran a lengthy investigation, Operation Anagram, to track Tobin's movements throughout his adult life in an attempt to tie him to unsolved crimes. It was wound down in 2011 but is still open and ready to probe any new evidence. As far as I know, the car park rape victim has still not had justice.

The strangest ID parade I ever arranged was in 1976 when I was based at Cranstonhill Police Office. A call came in to say a local nursery school had been hit by a kidnapping! Well, it was actually a hamster-napping.

The young pupils' favourite pet had been swiped from its cage in the classroom during a break-in and the weans were horrified and upset by the crime. Nothing else was stolen. The teacher had already done some detective work, asking the kids if they had any clues. A few of them said they had their own hamsters at home. One wee girl said her older brother had one too – he'd brought it to their house the previous evening.

DC McLaughlin was on the case. No need to dust for prints now – we had a prime suspect. The young teenager was well-known to me, as was his father, who was on first name terms with his local councillor, and through him regularly complained about the actions of the police.

I headed to the lad's home, happy to help out during a quiet period in my working week. When the father answered the door I stunned him by explaining I had a warrant to search for a hamster. The boy wasn't home so I started checking out the house, keeping my ears open for any rodent-like squeaks or creaking from a hamster's wheel. But there appeared to be no furry kidnap victims on the premises.

Just as I was leaving empty-handed, the front door opened and there stood the boy who was in the frame. Perched on his shoulder was a hamster. There was no coherent explanation from the boy about where he'd got his furry friend from. I didn't have a photofit of the hamster to hand but it matched the description of the missing teacher's pet. There was nothing else for it. I'd have to set up an official identification parade to get to the bottom of it.

Hammy was driven back to the station in my cop car and given comfortable accommodation in a plastic bin. I popped in some bread to keep it happy and put the lid on, ensuring the rodent was safe until we could arrange its star turn the next morning. But on my return I discovered we had an absconder on our hands. The toothy troublemaker had chewed its way to freedom and was now on the run in the police office. It was only a matter of time until it turned up and we knew what to expect when a high-pitched scream rang out later that afternoon. I ran to the scene and discovered the cleaner had found the hamster.

I headed to the local pet shop and borrowed six hamsters for the line-up. Of course they couldn't look too much like our one or completely different – that wouldn't be fair. I made my selection and invited the teacher to look for the classroom favourite. All the hamsters were placed together in a large box. We made sure it was metal so none of them could munch their way out. As they started scurrying around she picked out the one we suspected was hers and it was duly returned.

The boy who had sneaked into the classroom and pinched the creature was reported to the procurator fiscal for theft by house-breaking. I got a nice letter from Miss and the children thanking me for retrieving their pet. And I'm happy to say that for once I didn't hear anything about my handling of the case from the lad's father or his councillor pal. A good result all round.

10

THE SERIOUS CRIME SQUAD, ARMED AND DANGEROUS AND THE BODY IN THE TREE

Scotland's twenty city and county police forces were merged into eight regional services in May 1975. Strathclyde Police was born and that resulted in the creation of a new team of CID officers – the Serious Crime Squad. It replaced the old Flying Squad and took on the role of the 'heavy mob', called in to investigate the toughest of crimes. The squad had three teams, working on a 24-hour basis, headed by a detective inspector, with two detective sergeants and five detective constables. Each team had two cars to run about in.

I joined the squad in 1976. The worst area in Glasgow at that time was Barrowfield in the east of the city. It was lawless and all sorts went on there. One morning I was heading back to the office with a colleague after being at a would-be armed robbery that never happened. We decided to take a detour to visit one of the small tenement buildings in Barrowfield.

I had a tip that someone I was looking for was living at a particular address. My idea was to check out whose name was on the flat and store the information away for later. At the lower end of society, nameplates on doors were not in vogue. The occupants would scrawl their surnames in pencil on the whitewash of the close walls to ensure the postie could find them.

We parked discreetly round the corner and my fellow cop stayed in the car as I went exploring. Believing the man I wanted was on the top floor, I crept up the stairs. As I went up I heard some noise on the ground floor but didn't think much of it. Success! My target's name was written on the wall. That would come in handy for a future operation, I thought, as I headed back downstairs with a smile on my face.

I heard someone out the back and then I got a shock as I looked along the close to the entrance. There were two men lurking there. As I glanced at the back door, leading to the rear of the building, I saw another mean-looking individual blocking my path. I was in trouble. They didn't know I was a cop but they were obviously up to no good. It was common there for rent collectors or other people carrying money to be robbed.

At that point things took an even bleaker turn. One of the dodgy characters at the front was wearing a long coat. Suddenly, a large knife dropped from his sleeve into his hand. He turned round and eyed me menacingly. His companion also looked me up and down as if sizing up his kill, although I couldn't see a weapon on him.

There was nothing else for it. I drew my revolver, crouched and yelled, 'Armed police!' They were all taken completely by surprise and the shocked trio scattered. I took a moment to regain my composure but didn't bother chasing after them. Pulling a gun was a big deal, with the ensuing paperwork attached, so I never reported the incident. But having a Smith & Wesson handgun in your shoulder holster certainly came in handy on the mean streets of Barrowfield.

One of the villains of our acquaintance was William Elliot. His nickname was 'Toe' for some reason – perhaps because he was said to have turned-in feet. A wee guy, he nonetheless inspired fear. He'd become known as the Beast of the Gallowgate. Born in Calton, he kicked off his career as a gang leader as a youngster after his parents had separated. The violent crook's convictions included extortion, perverting the course of justice and a five-year stretch for drug possession. In 1975 he survived an assassination attempt after a row over the proceeds of a robbery. Two hoods tried to kill him by firing a gun through a letterbox but Toe escaped death and his attackers were jailed for life.

In 1976, we learned he was up to no good. Information suggested that Elliot and his henchmen were planning a raid in the city. The squad were given the task of tackling the situation. Nowadays, the police might contact the criminals in advance to warn them not to carry out their plans. But that wasn't our style. On the day, we kept a watch on the gang and saw them parking a vehicle with false plates and entering a business premises. But a huge removal lorry pulled up in the street just as the raid began, blocking in the getaway car. When Elliot and the others emerged after the theft, the driver could only hold his hands up in resignation and wave at them to scarper on foot.

Some of them headed off in one direction and Toe dashed off the other way, clutching a cash bag. We lost sight of him but we nabbed the other gang members. Then a call came in to say that an off-duty police officer needed some help not far away. When we arrived the cop was standing with his foot on Toe. He'd been sitting on a bus when he'd seen the suspicious character running down the street. He'd no idea who Elliot was but had chased him and tackled him to the ground. That stroke of luck had saved the day.

In December 1976, Elliot was sentenced to eight years for assault and robbery over the theft of £11,000, which was all recovered. But he didn't take it lying down. Although he admitted to the crime, he said his conviction should be reconsidered – because we had allegedly set him up. In May 1978, he and one of his co-accused, who got five years, kicked up a fuss. They wrote to the Secretary of State for Scotland complaining that an informant of one of my colleagues had arranged the entire raid. Elliot said he wouldn't have known about the rich pickings at the office if it hadn't been for the tout, who, he claimed, instigated the robbery looking to collect £2,000 from the cops for his help and info. The co-accused claimed he was a 'victim of circumstances'.

But Elliot served his time and, on his release, began to make his money from drug dealing. He and his henchmen brought violence and terror to the Glasgow drugs scene. Not surprisingly, he ended up in trouble again. In 1983 he was charged with the murder of one of his gang of pushers, Robert Kane. Feckless 34-year-old Kane had already had his arm smashed by drug dealers when he fell foul of Toe. He used some of the heroin he'd been supplied to sell and was unable to pay Elliot what he owed. After making threats, Elliot and another hood turned up at Kane's Maryhill flat wearing masks. They assaulted his junkie girlfriend and battered and stabbed Kane to death.

They tried to establish an alibi by going to a disco before and after the killing. But Toe was soon in the frame after witnesses identified him. He went on the run, robbing a bank in Riddrie with other crooks to fund himself. Shotguns were fired during the £57,000 raid and detectives pursued Toe in a car chase that ended with the hood crashing and being caught after a race through gardens and back courts. Toe was found guilty of the killing and given fifteen years. He admitted the bank robbery and was sentenced to twelve years. The diminutive gangster, wearing oversized glasses, was also convicted of dealing drugs and possessing a knife and a razor.

He ended up in the Barlinnie Special Unit, which did so much to turn around Jimmy Boyle's violent life. Toe was also a success story for the unit. He became a writer, penning a string of plays and setting up the Cat A theatre group with Boyle. He even wrote an episode of the TV show *Taggart*. Maybe I could have given him some story ideas for that one! After his release in 1999, he claimed the Beast of the Gallowgate was rehabilitated and vowed to go straight.

We were in Lanarkshire chasing a sex fiend in December 1976 when we got word of a horrifying crime that needed our immediate attention. Two inmates at Carstairs State Mental Hospital had broken out amid an orgy of violence, killing three people, and were on the run from the institution, which houses some of Scotland's most dangerous criminals. We were ordered to speed south and hunt the madmen.

We needed to be armed for our mission but were stymied. Officers in one of the other squad cars radioed with the bad news. They'd been into Hamilton Police Station to pick up weapons but had been refused. It was over a year since the merger of west of Scotland forces to form Strathclyde Police. But red tape was still a problem. Apparently the protocol to allow Glasgow detectives to pick up guns in Lanarkshire had not been put in place.

Our three squad cars lost vital time returning to Glasgow to get our guns. I was a DC, with three senior officers in the car, and, our apprehension growing, we headed to the Central Division to sign out our Smith & Wessons before getting on the road south amid increasingly wintry conditions.

Clutching our revolvers, each with twelve rounds of ammunition, our clapped-out motor roared down the icy A74 as the freezing temperatures closed in. We were updated by the dispatcher at police HQ. The murderous escapees were Robert Mone and Thomas McCulloch. Amid the crazed pair's flight, a Carstairs inmate, Ian Simpson, had been killed. So had a nursing officer, Neil MacLellan. Then a village police officer, George Taylor, had been hacked to death with an axe. Other members of the public had been injured by the fleeing duo.

Shocked by the details, especially knowing that a cop had been slaughtered, we drove on determinedly. Then a call came to switch our radio frequency to a secure channel. Suddenly, the voice of Chief Constable David McNee crackled into our cars. He repeated the horrifying news of the killings and assaults and then told us we must do everything in our power to ensure there was no further danger to the public from these desperate men.

Pausing to emphasise his point, he then said, 'Are you carrying?' We confirmed we had guns. The radio signal was poor so he asked again to be sure. 'Are you tooled up?' Our answer was again affirmative and he ended the call. It was up to us to interpret our instructions as best we could if we came face-to-face with the violent fugitives.

We continued our pursuit, aware the suspects were headed south on the A74 in a stolen car, heading for the border with England. But the weather conditions meant our car frustratingly lost radio contact with the other vehicles which were ahead of us. In the end, around Beattock Summit, we had to take desperate measures to keep in touch. We screeched into the car park of a nearby hotel and sprinted into the building to find a payphone. It must have shocked the patrons to see the red-faced foursome arrive.

HQ informed us we'd just missed the capture. Turned out the fugitives had got across the border before being apprehended. They'd wanted to be nabbed by the English police because, they said, they feared they'd be killed if they fell into the hands of armed Scottish detectives on a lonely road. They were assured they would have been unharmed if they'd given themselves up peacefully.

The brutal duo was taken to Carlisle Police Station where our men picked them up and drove them back north. We joined the convoy and got them back to Lanark Police Office. I remember being shocked by the sight of Mone. He was soaked from head to toe in his victims' blood.

At the High Court in Edinburgh in February 1977, McCulloch, aged 26, admitted murdering the three men and attempting to murder three others. Mone, a 28-year-old former soldier, pled guilty to killing PC Taylor.

They'd battled Mr MacLellan and their fellow patient in a recreation area. But the two men had fought back and been axed to death. The crazed pair had prepared the weapons for their escape along with a rope ladder and even a false moustache.

Outside, after using the ladder, and wearing nurses' uniforms, one of them had lain in the road until a car came along. The driver had got out to help the 'injured' man but a police car had drawn up at that point by chance. The pair had been angry when the motorist had told them the police would help and had sworn at him. They'd begun battling with the two officers and PC Taylor had been set upon by both as the driver had sped off to raise the alarm.

A bus had drawn up and the severely injured officer had been driven away for medical help. It was then, at about 7.20pm, that the victims in Carstairs had been found and it was discovered the two men were missing, Meanwhile, Mone and McCulloch had continued their mayhem. They'd stolen the police car and driven south, crashing at a crossroads and landing on an embankment with the blue light still flashing.

Two workmen had stopped to help but were brutally attacked with an axe and a knife and their van was stolen. Mone and McCulloch had travelled fourteen more miles through Biggar and crashed. At a farm at Roberton they'd terrorised the family who lived there. But the 12-year-old daughter showed remarkable bravery to slip away and phone the police.

The farmer's car was next to be stolen but the cops had caught up with the pair after they'd crossed the border and they'd been forced off the M6 onto a slip road, where they'd crashed. After hearing the horrific chain of events, the judge, Lord Dunpark, created a legal first when he sent them to prison for the rest of their natural lives.

The killer pair had been well-behaved patients at Carstairs until their carnage began. McCulloch had entered the hospital in

1970, ordered to be detained without limit of time after he'd admitted attempting to murder two people at the Erskine Bridge Motel in Renfrewshire. He'd gone there for a snack but had argued with staff – because there was not enough butter on his roll. He'd gone home for two shotguns, a revolver and ammo and headed back to the motel. He'd shot the chef through the cheek and blasted holes in bedroom doors before being over-powered.

His care in Carstairs was no use to him, according to psychiatrists who examined him before the 1977 trial, because he had an untreatable personality disorder. But hospital staff said they believed he was making steady progress before his rampage.

Mone had been locked up in Carstairs in 1968, the year after he had held up a classroom of schoolchildren in Dundee, raped one 14-year-old girl, sexually assaulted another and shot dead their pregnant teacher. Medical staff said he'd appeared to make slow progress but had improved by 1976. At his first trial he'd been ruled insane and unfit to plead but Carstairs doctors reckoned he was now sane.

During the months before the break-out he'd become editor of the hospital magazine, organised the drama society and worked hard in the joinery department. His lawyer said that, while they'd been organising their escape, he had tried to convince McCulloch that a minimum amount of violence should be used.

It was claimed they had broken out because they wanted to be put into the prison system, rather than returned to Carstairs, because they would eventually get a release date in jail.

Now that their plan to be moved had seemingly worked, there were concerns that other Carstairs inmates would resort to violence to achieve the same aim. The Prison Officers' Association said it was a genuine fear for the nursing staff. The Association added that the prison officers would now have to deal with the two men, who had little to lose as they were in jail for the rest of their lives.

But McCulloch's hope that he would possibly get a release date came to fruition in 2002 when he challenged his sentence under Human Rights law and had it fixed at 30 years. There was fury when he was given days out in 2011 amid speculation that he would be released on a life licence. The public vented their anger when he was seen in his native West Dunbartonshire and the Parole Board decided to keep him inside. However, he was moved to Noranside Prison in Angus where he continued to have days out, including in Dundee, where his partner in crime Mone committed his first murder.

As for killer and rapist Mone, he also won a 2002 legal fight to have a chance of parole and was moved to halfway house at Shotts Prison in 2011 to prepare him for a switch to an open jail. However, concerns about his behaviour saw him sent back to maximum security Glenochil Prison. The names of Mone and McCulloch continue to be among the most notorious in the annals of Scottish crime.

I was involved in more operations than I can remember over my career. A big investigation always needed a name, for easy reference. But you couldn't just slap on an obvious title, like Operation RBS for bank robberies. Big companies didn't like their names cropping up in the splash of publicity around police investigations. We were warned the Metropolitan Police in London had got into trouble with the name Operation Marks & Spencer, for instance.

The other no-no was a light-hearted name. There could be nothing jokey about the subject of the probe or too cute, such as Operation Angel. Could you imagine telling a grieving police widow her husband had lost his life in an operation with a daft name?

But that's not to say that humour couldn't be slyly injected into the titles. At one point we were chasing a group of post office raiders who were hitting their targets at night. They'd case the offices during daylight, always in a car belonging to one of the crew. As I sat around with my colleagues, mulling over suggestions for an inventive name for the op, one of our number piped up, 'How about Operation Delilah?' How come, we wondered? He said it was because of the car we were tracking – the one the crooks were using to cruise the joints. What about it? The make of vehicle wasn't relevant to the name Delilah?

What about the number plate, he pointed out. It took us a minute to recall what was on the licence plate – then we burst out laughing at his inventiveness. The last three letters of the plate were 'YYY'. That had instantly put him in mind of the Tom Jones song, with its well-known chorus, 'Why, why, why, Delilah?' We could have some fun despite the serious nature of the job.

The neds are always on the ball when it comes to keeping up with technology – and defeating it. That was particularly the case when the Police National Computer came into operation. The PNC stored vehicle details and could alert us immediately if a number plate or chassis number was from a stolen car or van. The crooks were a bit flummoxed by this for a while because, previously, they'd been able to hare about in a stolen car for a couple of days before news filtered through to the local cops to be on the lookout for the nicked motor.

They came up with all sorts of ruses to cheat the computer after it was introduced in the mid-1970s. One I remember tackling involved a spate of stolen cars that were mysteriously found with the boots burned out. The vehicles were all new, quality cars and were usually dumped on waste ground near the Partick Thistle football ground. Someone would always phone the fire brigade to report a vehicle ablaze and the firefighters would get there soon after. The fire was always started in the boot and hadn't been burning long so it was extinguished easily. That left the back of the car destroyed, the paint ruined and the interior damaged by smoke and flames.

But the front plate would be intact and the cops would quickly learn from the PNC that it was a stolen car and alert the owner, whose task it was to get the wreck removed. The owner would arrive to recover any property they'd left in the car and call their insurers to sort it out. Meantime, the local kids would further vandalise the burnt-out car, putting in the windows and stealing any good tyres that were left. The insurance company would decide the car was a write-off and arrange for it to be towed away. But that wouldn't happen quickly.

Eventually the cops worked out that there was a pattern to the thefts beyond where the cars were abandoned. In the period between the cars being dumped and taken away, their engines were stolen. They, of course, hadn't been damaged by the blaze at the back of the motor. That was no coincidence. They were new and valuable engines and it turned out getting hold of them was the whole reason for nicking the cars.

It was the neds who called the fire brigade to ensure the blazes were extinguished quickly to save the engines. The cars and their engines were listed in the PNC as recovered. So the engines were clean and the chassis numbers didn't come up as stolen. That way they could be stored for a while and then sold on to garages and fitted into other cars without any questions being asked. I got intelligence that the crooks had been running a couple of vanloads of expensive engines to Manchester and making a fortune. We set up an operation to intercept a future convoy of nicked engines – and put the sneaky trade off the road.

Another more elaborate method was outlined to me by an informant, who was giving me information about a bent auctioneer. A car sold at the auction would have a duplicate key which was passed to crooks by the corrupt auctioneer. After that they'd immediately steal the car during the night, knowing exactly where to find it because they had all the details from the auction. The neds would have already found an identical make and model of car and pinched it. A quick swap would be done.

Duplicate plates would be put on the second car and the mileage reset. All the personal property from the newly-bought motor would be transferred across to the stolen car and put in exactly the right place. Then the stolen car would be left outside the property where the auctioned car had been taken from.

The owner, unfamiliar with his new car, hopefully wouldn't notice that it wasn't the same vehicle. So the crooks were now driving about in a legitimate car which would not be registered as stolen. Meantime the innocent motorist was cruising in a duplicate vehicle with fake plates, unaware of the whole scam. I'm not sure how often the gang pulled this elaborate scam, but it was done with high-class cars and certainly was bold and inventive. They sent the car to another auction before the stolen car's tax expired, using the original purchaser's details.

Continuing to beat technology, the crooks found a way around remote locking in cars. They cut a tennis ball in half and put it against the key slot, battering it to send air pressure through the system to pop the locks. I told you they were on the ball! They also outsmarted the new police helicopter by driving getaway cars into tunnels and swapping rides out of sight of the eye in the sky. The chopper crew wouldn't see their target emerge and would have no idea which car to follow after the neds had switched vehicles.

One time, there was an amazing sight I never expected to witness – two men, sitting on a patch of rough ground, frozen solid. Human statues against the icy backdrop of Glasgow's Barlanark. I recall one was in his fifties, the other in his thirties. The pair had been strolling home from the notorious Caravel pub, owned by local gangster Tam McGraw.

They'd cut along a path that had been formed by people trudging across the waste ground. Their decision to take a wee break cost them their lives. Obviously, no one had spotted them as the freezing weather sucked the life from the pair and the grip of hypothermia turned to icy death. There they sat. One perched on a rock, the other on the ground. Had the booze caused them to drift into a fateful slumber? It was one for the medical experts. Try working out when rigor mortis had set in on those frozen corpses.

In his jacket, the older man had some identification so I tracked down his wife. She told me the younger man was a relative of her husband. She was too distraught to take up my offer to take her to the mortuary to identify the victims. We made sure she was being looked after by a friend and then asked her to get another relative to come to ID the victims.

We eventually worked out what had probably happened with the frozen men. The older chap had most likely taken a dizzy turn and needed to sit down. Why else would anyone take a rest in those inhospitable conditions? His companion had taken the weight off, too, to keep him company until he came round and could continue. Then the brutal winter weather had done its worst. It was a terrible sight and one I have certainly never forgotten.

Away from the pressures of the job, I always enjoyed bird-watching. It was a good way to relax. But I was on duty when I saw the queerest tree-dweller I ever came across. There, spread-eagled among the top branches, was a dead body.

I was called out to the crime scene in Springburn along with a Serious Crime Squad colleague. Perhaps the case of a man's body atop a tree was more appropriate for Special Branch, I thought, indulging in the black humour that was a way of coping with the tragic side of the job. It was a puzzler. How and why had someone disposed of their victim in such a bizarre and obvious way?

The tree body, lying in the branches on his back, had come as an even bigger surprise to the two ladies who had been strolling through a leafy area nearby with their pet dogs when they'd spotted the corpse. We tried to get some information from them but they didn't have a clue what had happened despite being regular walkers in the area.

In a bizarre twist on my usual habit of scanning trees for birdlife, I borrowed a pair of binoculars and peered at the body. He was stripped to the waist. What's more, his arms hadn't been affected by lividity – when blood pools at the lowest part of a dead body and discolours the skin. Because his arms were free from the blue colour that sets in, I was able to spot that he had tattoos on them.

That was a stroke of luck. The timing couldn't have been better because just the day before we'd had new guidance from the experts at the Scottish Criminal Record Office about identifying people through their body art. The SCRO said it had a new service, offering up a possible name if they were given the position and design of tattoos along with the person's stamping ground. Handy if you had a non-cooperative individual who wouldn't give up their name, and quicker than waiting for their fingerprints to be checked.

Gazing through my binoculars at the body in the tree, I realised I had a test for the SCRO boffins. I called them up and challenged them to try out their new system. I rattled off a description of the victim's tats, told them he was probably from Springburn, and waited for their verdict. Would he be in the system? The SCRO soon came back with good news. They had a name.

We checked it out and found out the guy was missing. Eventually he was identified formally and suspicion fell on one of his family members. It turned out the bizarre body dump had come about after the men had argued and the killer had struck. Then he'd decided to dispose of the corpse in a local landfill site, confident the victim's body would be covered over by tonnes of Glasgow garbage before anyone was any the wiser.

In dead of night, he'd slung the corpse over his shoulder and trudged through the dump, clambering up a steep pile of rubbish where the freshest landfill was being off-loaded. He'd heaved the body over the edge, reckoning it would plunge down the slope on the other side and be concealed when the landfill vehicles continued to tip in that spot. But, in the pitch black, he hadn't realised that there was an old tree in front of the pile of rubbish he was standing on.

When he'd thrown the body it had landed on top of the tree, resulting in the incredible revelation of the body in the branches when daylight arrived. The witnesses who'd spotted the body had been in a picturesque area of trees close to the dump.

It was a memorable discovery for all concerned and it fascinated me that the latest police techniques helped us solve the crime through the tattoos.

Sometimes investigating one crime can see you stumble upon a completely different one. Probing a murder in Springburn, I went door-to-door checking on all the residents in the close. One couple were away, apparently on their honeymoon in Spain.

I checked out the guy to try to eliminate him and found he had a minor warrant for breach of the peace. The address on the document was different from the one I'd visited. Intrigued, I headed to the Southside to check it out. A woman opened the door and I told her I was looking for the man as part of my inquiries. She confirmed he lived there but said he was away, working in England. She hadn't seen him for a while.

Then I noticed a wedding photo on the wall. It was her with her husband, who turned out to be the man I was looking for. Hang on, I thought, isn't he away on his honeymoon? It can't be the same person, I told myself. But he certainly matched the picture of the suspect on the warrant. 'Are you still married?' I enquired casually. 'Oh, yes,' she said. It looked like I had a bigamist on my hands! Not a crime I'd come across before and another one to tick off my list.

I headed off to make sure the guy had definitely married again and we confirmed he had. We picked him up with his new 'wife' at the airport when they returned from their holiday. It came as a total shock to her and she was devastated. I was surprised she didn't commit a breach of the peace when she found out. The two-timing Romeo was arrested for bigamy as well as the warrant offence. He had nothing to do with the murder.

Another house-to-house check had a similar lucky outcome. I was investigating a robbery and went to one home to ask routine questions. A woman welcomed me in and her partner immediately took my attention. He was sitting there – wearing sunglasses. That certainly made me suspicious. Nobody sports shades indoors unless they're a rock star or visually impaired. He was neither. Even more puzzling, it was the middle of winter. I reckoned he had something to hide. My interest piqued, I asked him a few questions. He gave me his name and said he was a student.

Back at the office I checked out the shady guy. It didn't surprise me to find out he had indeed been trying to keep a low profile behind his glasses. He was a prisoner who'd absconded from a jail in the north of England. He was soon back in the clink after we turned up again mob handed. He didn't see that coming – and not just because he was wearing sunglasses indoors.

New recruit
Bryan at Tulliallan
Police College.

Glasgow's Central Police
Office, where Bryan began
his career as a bobby.

PC McLaughlin's home from
home – a traditional Glasgow
police box.

A crash on Bryan's beat in the Gallowgate around 1967.

After his retirement from the police, Bryan became a private investigator and probed the alarming case of miscarriage of justice victim Stuart Gair.

Jimmy Boyle: a violent killer when Bryan first met him – by their next encounter Boyle was a reformed man and a talented sculptor.

The iconic portrait of notorious murderer Bible John. But Bryan fears it may not be an accurate likeness of the mysterious killer, who has never been caught.

Eccentric businessman Maurice Cochrane crossed Bryan's path before becoming embroiled in a sensational court case. DC McLaughlin was amazed by Cochrane's 'lie-detecting' toy elephant and his teddy bear, which was the 'personnel manager' of his firm, Rotary Tools.

Blonde Polish temptress Anna Grunt, who slept with Rotary Tools clients to win work for the company.

Bryan in 1978 when he was promoted to detective sergeant.

Was Scots serial killer Peter Tobin the rapist Bryan hunted in the mid-1970s? This photofit of the attacker led Bryan to believe they could be one and the same.

Glasgow was shocked when baby-faced killer Robert Tervet abducted 10-year-old Andrea Hedger as she walked to school and murdered her in an abandoned building.

Bryan tangled with John Friel, a suave Irish criminal who cruised Glasgow in a Rolls-Royce.

Michael Topham (looking at camera)
admitted murdering John Coughlan (left) and
burying his body in a lonely grave that has
never been found.

Edward Burke – known as 'Stab Eddie' – fired a Magnum handgun in a pub. The bullet killed one man and injured another.

Williamina Watson, aka Smoothie Susie. The scheming nurse used her bedside manner to con her way into the homes of elderly women and snatch their cash.

CAUTIONARY NOTE

An authorised Police Officer issued with a firearm in connection with his duties will be legally accountable for the consequences of its use and may require to satisfy a Court that its use against a person was justified due to imminent danger to life.

02/81

FIREARMS ACT, 1968.
AUTHORITY TO ENTER AND INSPECT

Name _____ BRYAN McLAUGHLIN

Regd. No. _____ 180631

is authorised in pursuance of the power conferred by Section 40(4) of the Firearms Act, 1968, or any subsequent legislation to the like effect, to enter any premises within the police area used by any person who, by way of trade or business, manufactures, sells or transfers firearms or ammunition for which a register is required to be kept and to inspect such register and all stock in hand.

Dated as overleaf.   Chief Constable

Bryan's authorisation to carry a firearm. Detectives had access to Smith & Wesson revolvers when tackling the most dangerous crooks and killers.

(Below) Bryan during his time as head of Criminal Intelligence, when he helped target gangster Tam McGraw (left) in a tax sting.

The Crimestoppers Scotland initiative was in danger of being discontinued until Bryan stepped in to take it over.

John McGeechan killed a man for throwing snowballs at his dogs. Bryan put him behind bars but he was later released and took another life.

Bryan met Nat Fraser to quiz him about the disappearance of his wife, Arlene. Fraser was later convicted of killing her.

Bryan on a holiday visit to the FBI headquarters in Washington DC.

11

COMMENDABLE ACTIONS AND
THE HIGH COURT BOMBED

One of the detective sergeants in the Serious Crime Squad got some alarming information in 1977. His informant told him four hardened East End criminals were planning to raid a factory in the city. Trouble was, he didn't know which business was to be targeted.

The tout passed on the date of the robbery and explained how the plan would work. They would steal a car and head to the factory, armed with baseball bats. Then they'd rob the staff wages as they were being delivered. I was sceptical of the flimsy details. If I had a pound for every time I'd lain in wait in vain for a crime to happen, I'd be richer than some of the crooks we hunted. This looked like another non-runner.

Nevertheless, on the day, we had squad cars staking out their homes in a bid to catch them early. But there was no sign of the four villains. The DS was back at the police station, hoping his informant would call with more details of the raid, but there was no word. We were in our surveillance van, positioned between a couple of factories where we gambled the robbers might strike. Of the eight detectives in the van, four, including me, were armed. Our Smith & Wesson handguns gave us a sense of security although we'd been told the gangsters would only have their bats to intimidate their victims.

Suddenly the police radio crackled into life. It was the DS with an update. The blag was on. He gave us the make, model, colour and registration of the stolen car. Then he passed on some information that made us very nervous. The four men were armed. But only two of them had baseball bats. The other pair had sawn-off shotguns! Any air of calm in the van disappeared when he confirmed he didn't know if the shooters were loaded.

Soon after, the stolen motor arrived and the tough-looking occupants jumped out and pulled balaclavas over their heads to disguise their identities. They headed for the entrance as the money had already been delivered. Four of us crept to the front door while the others went round the back. Inside, we heard threatening shouts and the sound of women screaming. Fortunately, there was no gunfire as the bandits scooped up the cash. We ran towards the commotion but our route was blocked by locked doors. Our colleagues had managed to get in and were now battling with the raiders.

At one point I looked through a window and saw one of our men tussling on the ground with a robber. They were both trying to get their hands on one of the shotguns. It was a frightening sight and I was desperate to help him before he got hurt. I spotted a door which had opaque glass in it. I tried to get it open but it was locked. Then I was met by the frightening vision, through the frosted glass, of a masked man advancing on the door with his shotgun raised.

He was obviously set on getting through the door to escape. Before I could react there was an almighty bang and I was engulfed in a wave of shattered glass. I saw blood dripping from my hands and my heart pounded as I realised I'd been shot. The crazed gunman must have used his weapon to blast though the locked door.

But I was still on my feet and had no time to check my wounds. The robber was staring through the broken glass, astonished to see a cop blocking his path. With a strength I never knew I had, probably driven by the surge of adrenalin, I grabbed him and pulled him through the door. My colleagues rushed to my aid and helped me slap handcuffs on the yelling crook.

I grabbed his shotgun and was surprised to see it was not loaded and hadn't been fired. To my relief, I worked out I hadn't been blasted with the gun after all. The massive bang I'd assumed was the shotgun being fired was the sound of the glass exploding as he'd used the weapon to smash in the window. The blood was mine, but only from cuts caused by the splinters of glass flying at me.

The three other men were also overpowered and their weapons were recovered. All the money was secured too. They went to the High Court in Glasgow and were each given ten years. Chief Constable Patrick Hamill awarded us all High Commendations for our part in thwarting the frightening crime. By the way, did I mention that when I got home on the day of the armed robbery, my underwear needed to be boiled twice?

Four trials were to be held over a series of armed robberies at hospitals and banks, allegedly masterminded by Glasgow crook Walter Norval. But on the eve of the start of the cases in October 1977, the High Court in Glasgow's Saltmarket was, incredibly, attacked with petrol bombs. The blaze damaged the north court in what was an apparent attempt to destroy files and evidence for the trials that were stored in the building.

I got an early morning phone call from my boss and I was soon at the scene of the crime with most of my Serious Crime Squad colleagues. The bombing was an incredible affront to Scottish justice. We were determined to find the hoods who had tried to bring the historic court building down in flames and show them they couldn't neuter justice.

Fortunately, the attempt to halt the trials was a failure and the band of crooks was hauled in front of four judges and four juries. Their names were kept secret from the public during the proceedings. Some say that's why they became known as the XYY Gang. Others claim the name is something to do with police radio code. After the outrageous attack, security was at a maximum and I was among armed officers who guarded the judges on their way to and from court and stayed outside their accommodation in the city.

I was also on the hunt for the petrol-bombers. One man who was put under the spotlight was David Garvie, a 32-year-old crane driver from the Temple area. Along with a senior collea-gue, I turned up at his home to look for him. His wife claimed he wasn't there but we noticed a shape under the blankets in a bed recess. I pulled the bedding aside and there was Garvie. He gave me a false identity – Willie Johnston, the name of a footballer. It was suspicious behaviour indeed.

I had an interesting encounter with another person in the household. She was a relation of Garvie and the wife of a character called Joe Polding – one of Walter Norval's henchmen. Polding was among those facing charges in the XYY trials. Mrs Polding, who had a baby in her arms, asked me how long I reckoned her husband would be sentenced to if found guilty. I said the child would likely be married by the time he was released. 'He won't be out for a generation,' I advised her. 'How long is that?' she demanded. I told her I thought her man would get 25 years and she looked shaken. It wasn't my last interaction with Mrs Polding.

We searched Garvie's car and found some interesting evidence – a knotted rope, a lemonade bottle containing liquid, an oil can with petrol in it, a tin of cellulose thinner and other items. We charged him with the court bombing. Rita Gunn, Norval's daughter, and her husband, William, were also accused of conspiring to bomb the court.

Back at the XYY trials, after three weeks of courtroom drama, seven men were acquitted before the verdicts came in on the remaining six, including Norval. Just before the jury gave their pronouncement, I was in a room in the court with fellow detectives. Suddenly, a well-known member of the press rushed in uninvited. 'Quick, lads,' he panted. 'What's Walter Norval's nickname?' He obviously wanted a catchy title to put in the paper when the crook was inevitably found guilty and could finally be identified in the media.

We looked at each other in silence. Norval didn't have a nickname. Indeed, we weren't in the habit of giving them to criminals. Names like Bible John were inventions of the press, as was the one given to Chief Constable David McNee – The Hammer. He'd never been called that but he didn't object to the image it portrayed.

One of my colleagues, who knew the pressman, told him convincingly, 'He's known as "the Godfather".' The hack's face lit up and he sprinted off in delight.

'The Godfather! Where did you get that one from?' I asked the other cop.

'Ach well,' he said. 'The name Norval sounds a bit Italian so that will do.'

And that's how Norval came to be known by the legendary nickname, which led the press to characterise him as a Mafia-style ringleader of organised crime.

Norval, a 49-year-old grandfather, was jailed for fourteen years and his gang, described by the press as 'Scotland's first big-time crime syndicate', got sentences ranging from twenty-one to four years. Among them was Joe Polding, the man whose wife I'd run into at Garvie's place. He admitted raiding the city's Leverndale Hospital and the Glasgow Savings Bank in Milngavie. His lawyer told the trial that he was a married man who had only got involved because he'd got into debt to illegal moneylenders who'd forced him to take part. The former shipyard worker said threats were made to his family to get him to cooperate and he'd been told that no violence would be used in the robberies, for which he earned £700. He claimed to be a mere pawn who'd been caught up in the crimes through a combination of greed and fear for his family.

When he was sentenced to 18 years, Mrs Polding turned round to me in the public benches and told me, 'See, you were wrang!

He didnae get twenty-five years. He only got eighteen!' That's what's called looking on the bright side! I didn't tell her another of my sentence estimates had been more accurate. I won the sweepstake run by the cops with my guess that the gang would get 74 years in total. I scooped a bit of cash for that one.

The trial over the High Court bombing was held in February 1978. But it wasn't just the explosives attack that was alleged. Charges of witness intimidation related to the XYY case were also made against Rita Gunn and her husband, who were said to have put the frighteners on witnesses and a couple of my police colleagues. Another man, John McNeil, who'd been found not guilty of armed robbery during the XYY trials, was accused of threatening witnesses due to give evidence against Mrs Gunn.

Forensic expert Dr William Rodger told the jury he had examined the rope we'd discovered in David Garvie's car and found fibres sticking to it. They matched fibres from red gloves found at the scene of the court bombing. But Garvie insisted he had used the rope to tie a suitcase to his car. He claimed he and his wife had red woollen pullovers similar to the fibres found and the rope had been used to hang out clothes. He insisted he had an alibi for the night of the fire. He'd been at a Rangers social club with pals. Recalling our arrival at his door, he said he'd thought we were men from the social security and had given a fake name. Garvie broke down in the dock at one point, claiming the stress of the trial was too much for him. William Gunn also began weeping.

Then there was the witness intimidation. I had a taste of it myself while investigating the threat claims. I went to speak to a suspect. When I left I checked my car, as I always did, and noticed someone had put six-inch nails in front of my tyres to burst them. Suffice to say, after that I paid a few extra visits with my colleagues to the individuals suspected of being behind it.

It was claimed in court that a garage owner and his wife had been threatened because they had refused to say that Norval's car had been at their business premises at the time it was seen at one of the XYY gang robberies. The garage boss alleged McNeil had told him there was a threat to his life, then William Gunn had phoned him and warned, 'They'll catch up with you some time and fill you full of holes.'

The garage owner's wife and detectives claimed 28-year-old Mrs Gunn had made threatening remarks to them before her father's trial. But she was acquitted of those charges and of conspiring to destroy the court. Her husband was also found not guilty over the court blaze but was given five years for witness intimidation. McNeil was convicted of issuing threats and sentenced to four years. In the end, no one was done for the brazen attack on the court. Garvie, the man accused of climbing onto the roof to start the fire, walked free when the charge was found not proven.

Rita Gunn said afterwards she was annoyed her father was now being called the Godfather. She complained, 'It was the police who gave him that name.' Well, she was kind of right. The garage boss praised the squad for protecting him and his family but said he was thinking about leaving Britain because he still feared repercussions.

Another man considering quitting Glasgow was David Garvie, who said he and his wife wanted to escape the notoriety of the trial. 'The last fifteen weeks have been bloody murder – a nightmare,' he told the press. Joe Polding served 11 years and was released in 1989. His boss, Walter Norval, was out after nine years.

127

12

FINGERPRINTING A TOWN
AND THE KILLING OF A CHILD

Three cars packed with Serious Crime Squad detectives headed through freezing conditions from Glasgow to Ayrshire. Based at Temple Police Station, we were racing out of town to probe another in the litany of west of Scotland murders we investigated over the years.

Alongside me in the car was the rest of the four-man team – another detective constable as well as a detective sergeant and a detective inspector. It was December 1977 but there was not much festive cheer as we rumbled on over the wintry moors. We'd been told we'd be down there until the crime was solved so we were preparing for a long haul. At least the overtime would come in handy.

In Girvan, Ayrshire, a café owner had been found dead in a pool of blood in the storeroom of his premises. Enrico Iannarelli had been stabbed to death in a violent attack – with two knives. Cops had discovered a number of fingerprints in blood. It was like something out of a mystery movie but they were a vital clue to a brutal killing.

We tried out a first in Scotland – fingerprinting a whole town. It was an ambitious plan to find suspects for the killing, which had baffling aspects. If it was a robbery, why was over £15,000 cash found in the victim's safe along with jewellery and foreign currency?

And what had happened to his little black book? It was a list of customers he'd always kept in his top pocket. Some said it was a record of people he'd given credit. But rumours swirled around that Mr Iannerelli had been involved in moneylending and his book was a potentially embarrassing record of clients. That was something his wife denied. Perhaps someone out there had more on their mind than robbery when they took the café owner's life.

The big fingerprinting operation swung into action in mid-January. The unusual move had been agreed after consultation with the Crown Office. Police numbers on the case were doubled to 80. Over about six days, officers knocked on the doors of the 7600 residents to get prints from about 5000 of them – every man, woman and child over the age of 14. Of course, it was voluntary. But those who had nothing to hide had nothing to fear and there were few objections, as I recall.

Because some would be out of town over the weekend, the murder HQ in Girvan was opened up to allow them to come in for printing to ensure they weren't missed out of the elimination process.

As we went knocking door-to-door, we established who lived there and arranged for them to be fingerprinted, sometimes carrying out the job ourselves. But the squad was primarily there as the investigative hub and others were carrying the burden of printing not only the residents but also workers. Factory staff who came into town for employment were checked as well as locals.

On our house-to-house inquiries, I got myself into trouble. At a large, posh home I encountered the lady of the house, who was obviously a local worthy of some sort. She was apparently aghast at all these bobbies tramping about her wee town and quizzed me on where I was from. When I mentioned Glasgow, she became very snooty about my beloved city.

I listened as she ran down the rougher areas, telling me how awful they were. I must be seeing a different side of life now I was out in a quiet seaside town, she suggested. I'd bitten my lip long enough and decided to put her straight about her opinions. Explaining that I'd seen every corner of Girvan on my trek around the streets, I informed her that the number of people who were socially deprived in her wee town was as large, if not larger, per head of population, than some of the tough areas of Glasgow.

She took great offence at the apparent slur and complained about me to a senior officer. Asked to explain my forthright comments, I told the brass that I had seen a frightening amount of poverty among the locals. A couple of our lads had even been involved in a scabies scare, I pointed out. One house had a chopped-up tree inside a bedroom to be used later as firewood, I recalled.

But the incident that put the tin lid on it came when I was checking one home and found an unexpected sight in the bath – a donkey! The silly asses who owned it had nowhere else to keep it so they stuck it in the tub with some hay to keep it going. The donkey had access to water and its mess could, in part, be flushed away down the plug.

It was a bizarre discovery – I've no idea why they had it. It's unlikely they were offering donkey rides on the beach. No more was heard about the woman's comments after I'd outlined my views.

Eventually, a fingerprint helped us focus in on a set of local suspects – the Foote family. Margaret Foote, who was 48, had previously worked for Mr Iannarelli and was thought to be on good terms with him. A bloody print on a door matched her.

It seemed that more than one person had been involved in the attack and our spotlight fell not only on Mrs Foote, but also on her husband, 49-year-old George, and their daughter Yvonne, who was 21.

Ready to pounce, we all gathered in a local hotel the night before the big op. Over a small drink to keep us calm, the boss laid out our duties. My task was to arrest hubby. Early next morning, while my colleagues headed off to find the wife and daughter, I motored back out of town. My information was that

Mr Foote was staying in the Glasgow area at that point. Perhaps he had cleared out of Girvan amid the rumours sweeping round.

When my quarry came to the door I had to suppress a smile. He was smoking a pipe. Nothing unusual in that, you might think. But I couldn't believe I was nabbing a pipe-smoker – for murder.

Only a few days before, a police colleague, who enjoyed puffing his baccy, had insisted to me that he'd never nicked a pipe-smoker and was sure he never would. His theory was that anyone with the good sense to enjoy clamping a calming pipe between his teeth was a steadfast, dependable, solid citizen. So much for that idea! Or maybe I should just have pronounced my suspect innocent there and then. He was a respectable-looking wee guy but, as a DC, I wasn't privy to the ins-and-outs of all the evidence. It didn't help the family's cause that money from the café was found in the loft of their home.

Along with his wife and daughter, he was charged with stabbing the victim to death, stealing around £3,000 from the safe and trying to set the café on fire by pouring paraffin or a similar fluid over the dead man's clothing.

In a bizarre description of events given to cops, George Foote said he'd gone to bed alone on the night the victim had died and his wife, who was suffering from a headache, had stayed up. Waking later to find Margeret Foote was not there he had checked with daughter Yvonne. She'd gone looking for her mum and seen a light on in the café. But she'd been stunned when she'd looked through the window and seen Mr Iannarelli lying on the floor.

Mr Foote said his daughter had alerted him and he'd rushed to the café, where he'd worked part-time, and been met with a frightening scene. His wife was standing near the victim's body. She'd claimed he'd tried to rape her, Mr Foote said. In his version of events, he'd staggered from the building, his head swimming, assuming Mr Iannerelli was merely unconscious.

He'd gone to bed and, when his wife had come back and asked what she should do, he'd said it was her problem. His claims

131

contrasted with those of his wife, who said she'd gone to visit a friend that night and found the victim's body when she'd called in at the café.

At the trial of the family in April 1978, Mr Foote's statement was heard and the judge instructed the jury to return a verdict of not guilty in relation to him and his daughter. There were emotional scenes as the sobbing father and daughter left the court.

The charge against Mrs Foote was modified to remove a reference to previous malice and ill-will allegedly shown by her to the dead man, and the amount she was accused of stealing was reduced to £2,500.

Margaret Foote was found guilty by a majority and jailed for life for what the judge described as 'a very cruel and brutal murder'. But the press pointed out the judge had reeled off a number of mysteries thrown up by the six-day trial.

Why had money been left? What happened to the little black book? Who was the unidentified scar-faced man who twice turned up at an Ayr chippie with a girl and paid with blood-stained notes? Also, a woman and two men had been seen talking to the victim after opening hours on the night of his death. Another mystery man, a bushy-haired individual, had turned up on the doorstep of the dead man's widow only about 30 minutes after her husband had died.

The papers also pointed out that there were a number of unidentified bloody fingerprints at the scene of the hideous killing of a man who was known as a respectable member of the seaside town and a benefactor of the Catholic Church.

It was a measure of the force's dedication to finding the culprit that we went to the remarkable lengths of getting dabs from an entire town in our pursuit of justice.

There is something particularly horrifying about a young child going missing. In my day, the term 'paedophile' wasn't really in common use. But everyone knew that men who wanted to abuse children stalked the streets and, more often, caused heartache within their own families. For cops who were parents, it was particularly difficult to deal with these cases.

It was April 1978 when 10-year-old Andrea Hedger went missing in the Woodside area of Glasgow on her way to school. She was running late after her parents had slept in and she was clutching a note for the teacher explaining her tardy arrival. But she never made it to Willowbank Primary.

There was immediate consternation when it was realised she was lost. The little girl with the 'Purdey' haircut – copied from the character on TV show *The Avengers* – was known to be keen on school and her family said she would have rushed to get there rather than going off somewhere. A massive search began but nothing was found on that first day.

It was an agonising three days for Andrea's parents and the community as the mystery continued. But then their worst fears were realised. In a derelict building in Ashley Street – a rough area frequented by lowlifes – cops searched a dingy, dark basement. It was a haunt of drug users and young girls who prostituted themselves on a dirty mattress on the floor. There, the officers made a horrible find.

In the dungeon they noted a pile of wood topped off with a cut-out image of a red dragon. They pulled the rubbish aside and there, on the grotty mattress where the street girls plied their seedy trade, was the body of little Andrea. She'd clearly been sexually assaulted and strangled with her own scarf. As the locals yelled for the killer to be caught, the force threw all its resources at the investigation, launching one of the biggest murder hunts ever seen at the time.

I was among the sixty detectives who were on the task force. There was a good response from the public – including those who inhabited the twilight world of crime. The shocking nature of the killing meant prisoners sent letters from jail offering information. Crooks and prostitutes cooperated with us. An

133

astonishing dossier of local crime was built up by the police blitz. Within a couple of days, two cases of rape and one of sodomy that had not previously been reported were discovered. Dozens of more minor matters like thefts and break-ins were cleared up as the culprits confessed to keep suspicion away from them in the murder case. We also got vital intelligence about a number of young girls involved in prostitution in the area.

Hard work and intuition led to a suspect being identified. Not a hulking, mean-looking brute but a 'baby-faced' teenager. Robert Tervet, a 19-year-old who lived in the shadowy world of the Woodside underground, had been interviewed before about a sexual assault. His story hadn't been convincing and now we wanted to talk to him about Andrea. It was discovered that, suspiciously, he had left Glasgow and a warrant for his arrest was issued over an earlier theft of lead he was linked to. Turned out he'd gone south to visit relatives and moved on to Manchester, where Tervet had spent time enjoying the nightlife. He was eventually picked up on April 21 and allegedly said to cops, 'This is about the murder isn't it? I want to tell you about it.'

Back in Glasgow, I encountered Tervet when he was detained at Cranstonhill Police Office. He agreed to provide a voluntary statement – a confession – to the arresting officers. Now a thing of the past, voluntary statements were taken under strict rules. The guidelines insisted that they could only be used in evidence if they were given unprompted by police questioning. An accused had to be cautioned and advised they could have a lawyer before they could give a voluntary statement. If they'd already spoken to a solicitor, they had to consult again with their brief before we could take the statement. It would be noted in writing and was tape-recorded after that technology was introduced.

I arranged for his clothing to be taken for forensic examination. Tervet showed no remorse, only self-pity. His twisted version of events was that Andrea had approached him to offer some sympathy because she'd seen him weeping in the street. He was crying over an argument with his under-age and pregnant girlfriend, a 15-year-old schoolgirl prostitute who'd been his only serious relationship. He said he'd seen a love-bite on the girlfriend's neck.

Tervet claimed Andrea had asked, 'Mister, why are you crying?' But her parents denied she would have gone up to a stranger in that way, especially when she was late for school. Describing her throughout his statement as 'the wee lassie', Tervet revealed he'd given her sweets. The sick teenager said he'd somehow imagined Andrea was the girlfriend and decided to take his brutal revenge, leading her to the basement where he'd raped and strangled her.

Unemployed Tervet was one of a family of eleven and had nearly a dozen previous convictions. He came from a deprived background, his mother having died in 1970. His father was living in a hostel and had little to do with his son. Most other family members had moved to England. He'd lost a job as a van boy at the fruit market aged 16 and had turned to petty crime, like theft and housebreaking. He'd ended up in borstals, hostels or living rough in the hidden world of the West End. He'd met up with his girlfriend while they were both homeless but the pregnant teen, due to give birth in a few weeks, was now devastated by his arrest and was under medical care.

Although he was of low intelligence and had a personality disorder, he was judged sane and fit to plead by psychiatrists. At the High Court in Edinburgh that June, Lord Wheatley was told Tervet was living in fear in the hospital wing at Barlinnie Prison due to threats from other prisoners who had made him a marked man under their strange code of ethics that dictated that sex offenders were the lowest of the low. There had also been rumours, Tervet's counsel said, that his client had mutilated the girl's body. Although it wasn't true, the cons had come to believe it.

The judge got himself into some trouble with his response. He told Tervet, 'It may be that you will suffer in prison for the nature of your crime but, having regard to the nature of that crime, I can feel no sorrow for any treatment to which you may be subjected.' That later sparked condemnation from prison reform groups who felt it was the wrong message to give inmates. Lord Wheatley added that the English language didn't contain sufficient descriptions for Tervet's actions and the law didn't have adequate punishments for what he'd done to Andrea. He gave Tervet life with a minimum sentence of 15 years. He also imposed 10 years' detention in a young offenders institution for the rape and 12 months for the theft of lead, worth £250.

The case turned the spotlight on Woodside, revealing part of it as a red light area where criminals lived in a shadowy realm of the city. But locals in the multi-ethnic enclave were outraged to be tarred with that brush and said it only applied to a clutch of streets there. They admitted parts such as Ashley Street, Grant Street, Carnarvon Street and Baliol Street, where Andrea lived, had become run-down and were haunted by drifters, pimps and prostitutes. The local MP said the blight of prostitution had been known about for years but government money was needed to tackle the problem in Woodside, which was already undergoing environmental improvements. It was an area I knew well and often visited during my professional duties. A once salubrious place brought down by the letting and sub-letting of properties.

Tervet's former girlfriend had their baby and gave it up for adoption before running away to London. Incredibly, she lived there with another man who went on to be arrested and convicted for murder. She was given residential training for a year after being caught working the streets and, as her release approached, decided she wanted her baby back. But a sheriff decided in November 1979 that the girl, from Nitshill, wasn't fit to look after the child and the tot remained in the care of foster parents. Perhaps the mother's choice of budding murderers as her partners didn't help her cause!

As for Tervet, he survived his incarceration despite all those inmates he claimed were out to get him. He was transferred to Liverpool Prison and towards the end of his sentence moved to Leyhill open jail in Gloucestershire. He was released by the Parole Board in 1997, and the last I heard he was living in the south of England.

13

THE SCOTTISH CRIME SQUAD, SURVEILLANCE SKILLS AND TRAVELLING CRIMINALS

In 1978, I was promoted to Detective Sergeant and was among a group of officers seconded to the Scottish Crime Squad. With offices in Glasgow and Edinburgh, the squad's remit was to follow travelling criminals across Scotland, either to find out where they lived or to arrest them. We moved throughout the country to probe major crimes or, when not called on by one of the eight Scottish forces, we trawled criminal haunts for information.

Following targets was an expensive operation as tracking each one required five specially constructed cars with at least two officers in them. Courses were run in both foot and car surveillance techniques. Some sneaky criminals sent people to take a note of the registration numbers of our undercover cars when we parked at the police office. We swapped vehicles regularly with other cops and used 'ghost plates' to alter our licence numbers.

Tricks like going round roundabouts several times, turning on main roads or suddenly stopping, meant some crooks were very hard to follow. Tracking devices were used on some target vehicles when special permission was granted. We once got a new tracker to test and took it out for a ride, noting it worked well. Putting it through its paces a bit more, we clamped it to the bottom of one officer's car without telling him. We tracked him to Edinburgh – where he visited a sauna! No more was said about the matter.

A surveillance-aware target was difficult to follow but not impossible. We had a change of clothes in the car. Sometimes we had two people in the front, sometimes one would lie down in the back seat to vary the number seen. Female officers could wear wigs to change their appearance. We could swap male and female drivers over.

Each 'eyeball' car – the one in front – would only take the lead for a short time, then drop back to become 'tail-end Charlie'. Some of our vehicles had hidden cameras fitted around the headlamps, worked by remote control, to get video footage of our prey. The cameras even moved to stay level depending on the camber of the road. Some of our vehicles looked clapped out but actually had brand-new engines. Our best car for the centre of Glasgow was an inconspicuous Black Hack taxi.

Sometimes things didn't go to plan, like the occasion the Glasgow-based squad targeted a local criminal and ended up in Edinburgh. Because they were unfamiliar with the streets they lost him. On the same day the Edinburgh team followed one of the capital criminals and found their way to Glasgow. They got lost too.

Another top target made a point of never parking his car immediately outside his house. He'd been watched several times before and kept a note of as many of our cars as he could. He was also suspicious of every van in his street as he knew we used them to observe his movements to and from his close and spot any associates he had. He realised we had officers in them for a long period of time.

The vans had heating and catering and toilet facilities and could be parked near a target's house for up to eight hours or more before he was likely to leave his home. After an all-night watch on this man's tenement flat, he was spotted leaning out of his window and surveying all the cars and vans in sight. Satisfied he was not being watched, he left his house and made for his car. We grabbed him in a successful swoop. But he was livid at being caught because he prided himself on being able to outwit our watchers.

Back at the police station, he let us know how on-the-ball he thought he was. He suddenly told us the number of our sur-veillance van, which we'd used while tracking him. He was right although we didn't confirm it to him. Asked why he thought it was that vehicle, he explained the snowy weather had tipped him off as he'd looked from his second-floor home. Every vehicle in the street had snow on its roof that morning – apart from our van. He now realised that was because of the bodies inside creating enough heat to melt it.

His tip caused us more expense as our surveillance vans had to have their roofs 'double skinned' to stop heat escaping and melting any covering of snow in future.

Another time, my hobby of collecting currency helped us crack a crime. We arrested a man we'd been tracking over some housebreakings. In his possession, I found an American two-dollar bill. I knew from my interest in the subject that $2 notes were extremely rare so we were able to trace it back to the owner to link the suspect to a robbery.

We had a great success at one point, cracking a theft of a cigarette lorry in Paisley and recovering tens of thousands of stolen cigarettes and other nicked gear as well as the vehicle, which added up to over £100,000.

We were told the crooks had found an unused unit on an industrial estate. The electricity was shut off in the building but they'd been able to break a small window and open the large sliding door using the manual override. It was the ideal hiding place for the lorry, which couldn't be seen in the dark building from the outside. We recovered the cigarettes – all but one box – and other items the truck was carrying.

Eventually, we heard from the grateful insurance company, who had promised a reward for information resulting in the arrest and conviction of the perpetrators. It was one of my informants who'd given us vital intelligence that had helped solve the crime. The insurers were keen to pay a 10 per cent fee – a hefty £10,000. That seemed reasonable to me after such a big success. They intended sending a cheque to our office to pass on to the informant. But I didn't want to get directly involved in the process as it was my man who was being rewarded so I insisted that the insurance company should send a representative to Glasgow to meet with a senior officer on the squad to deal with the cheque. But when the other cop got involved problems began to surface. He was from one of the smaller forces and perhaps hadn't had much experience of handling big cases like that one.

'I think handing over that kind of money to an informant is morally wrong,' he informed me. Perhaps he was wary of the public finding out about characters that moved in underworld circles profiting from information they picked up about nefarious goings on. I couldn't argue too much as he outranked me, so I left the matter at that and let him get on with it. In anticipation, the informant opened a bank account – in a false name. The cheque was given to the tout but, unknown to me, he only got £5,000. Cue an angry phone call from my informant about the 'measly' pay-out he'd been given after putting himself at risk by divulging information about the crime.

I told him I hadn't had a role in it but he wouldn't be placated. 'I expected at least ten per cent as my reward,' he barked. 'That's it. I've had it with you lot. You're getting nothing more from me.'

Sadly, he was as good as his word. The flow of information from an important informant stopped after that. So the senior officer was indirectly responsible for halting my relationship with one of my best touts. The crook went onwards and upwards in the criminal world and ended up as an international jewel thief. Think of all the tip-offs he could have given me!

I organised criminal intelligence, unofficially, within the Scottish Crime Squad between 1979 and 1982. They didn't have a dedicated

Criminal Intelligence section until the late 1980s. I became adept at pinpointing criminals from their habits and mannerisms. At one stage Rangers Football Club went to play a match in Belgium, which coincided with a large theft of jewels from a shop in the country, suspected to have been carried out by Scots crooks. The Belgian cops called the squad for advice and any tips on who could be behind it. They told me the gang had booked into a fancy hotel under false names. I had a thief in mind so I instructed the *gendarme* to go up to the rooms and check the beds. He must have thought I was daft. But I explained that if one of the mattresses was soaked in urine, I'd name that crook in one. Turned out exactly that had happened and we knew immediately who we were looking for. The thief was renowned for leaving his unusual calling card. He didn't wet the bed. He always deliberately urinated on the mattress wherever he was staying. Who knows why but it helped nab him.

After another jewellery theft, this time in the Wick area, we were sent security camera footage of the raid. The crooks' faces couldn't be seen clearly but one of them gave his identity away to the trained eye. He was a man who always rubbed his hands together in anticipation as the loot was about to be given to him. The Wick robber did exactly that when the jewels were passed to him. Case closed.

I remember my commander was present on two occasions when a telex came in with details of a crime and I was able to name the crook immediately based on my knowledge of their methods and activities. That hopefully made a good impression on him and I think it all helped to build a good career.

In February 1979, we were alerted to two explosions in city pubs within 15 minutes. Had Irish terrorism come to Glasgow's streets? That was certainly our fear. The first Saturday night blast was at the Old Barns in London Road, near the Barras. It was known as a hang-out for Irish exiles. The second apparent bombing was at the Clelland Bar in Hospital Street, Gorbals – a pub that wasn't considered linked to Irish Republicanism despite being in a heavily Catholic area.

As other squad colleagues made for the Old Barns, I headed to witness the mayhem at the Clelland Bar, where five of the 32 people in the pub had been injured. I was relieved to hear their wounds were not life-threatening. One had a broken ankle and the others had been hit by flying glass from windows and the damaged jukebox and fruit machine. But that didn't take into account the trauma of finding yourself in the middle of a bombing while enjoying a Saturday night out.

Special Branch were on the scene, too, as we surveyed the wreckage and began an elaborate operation. Army bomb squad experts arrived from Edinburgh to look for clues about the explosion. Shards of shattered glass, pieces of broken furniture and other debris were collected for thorough examination. The clothing of the blast victims would be recovered later to be probed.

The bar at the Clelland had been wrecked by the explosion. People could easily have been killed. The publican said the sudden blast had come from one side of the pub and he'd been knocked off his feet. Having seen an orange flash, he'd assumed it was an electrical explosion. A barman said he'd been collecting glasses when the blast had sent him diving to the floor along with customers. He recalled a gantry had collapsed, which had probably injured some customers. A young woman described how she'd been leaving when the drama had happened. She'd been thrown off her feet and was suffering from burns, cuts and bruises on her legs – but realised it could have been much worse for her. No one had been hurt at the Old Barns, where the explosion went off in a lounge that was being redecorated and was empty.

It was quickly established that the blasts had, as feared, been caused by explosive devices and that an extremist group was probably behind the attacks. Within a couple of days fifteen men were in custody following a police swoop on various homes in the city by the Serious Crime Squad and Special Branch. The armed cops arrested them under the Prevention of Terrorism Act and had an initial 48 hours to question the suspects.

A mobile police station was set up outside the Clelland Bar as our inquiries continued. Meanwhile, Chief Constable Patrick Hamill warned the public to be on their guard in pubs and clubs. They should show 'utmost vigilance', he advised, and report any suspicious people or packages and holdalls that were unattended.

Eventually ten men were charged and a massive security operation was needed for their unusual court hearing. They were not taken to Glasgow Sheriff Court because of fears over the situation so a huge op was mounted at Stewart Street Police Station in Cowcaddens, which became a specially-convened court for the occasion. Armed cops surrounded the building and police marksmen watched from rooftops as the suspects arrived.

Police cars sealed off the front and back entrances and officers patrolled the nearby high flats. After a short hearing, the men were driven to Barlinnie Jail flanked by ten police motorcyclists and two cop cars. The suspects' high-profile lawyers, Joe Beltrami and Ross Harper, complained that the security operation was an 'over-reaction' that brought unhelpful publicity to their clients and could influence a future jury.

By the time of the trial in May, eleven men who were allegedly members of the outlawed Ulster Volunteer Force were in the dock. They appeared, under heavy security, at the High Court in Glasgow charged with acquiring guns and money over four years to further the cause of the UVF. They were also charged with the pub bombings. Almost 400 witnesses were lined up for the trial.

One of the Clelland barmen told the jury of a sherry-drinking stranger with a bag who was in the pub on the night of the blast. He said the man's unlikely choice of drink had drawn attention to him. He was identified as one of the accused men, Angus

McKenna. The pub worker said McKenna had been carrying the bag over his shoulder and had wandered over to watch some of the regulars playing pool and to look at the jukebox.

The witness said McKenna, whose fingerprint had been found on a broken glass after the crime, had left the pub at 9.45pm – twenty minutes before the bomb went off. Another man the barman didn't know had been in the pub that night and had been notable because of the speed at which he'd downed a couple of pints before leaving. The barman, who insisted the pub wasn't a 'sectarian' bar, couldn't identify the mystery man among the accused.

At the end of the trial, nine of the UVF gang were found guilty and jailed for between 12 and 18 years each. Four were convicted of the bombing offences and received the heaviest punishments. McKenna was given 18 years for each of the bombing charges and a total of 48 years on five other charges. The other bombers were given 16 to 18 years for their part in the explosions.

Another of the jailed men was Bill Campbell. The 39-year-old was given 16 years in jail for contravening the Explosive Substances Act. On other charges, his sentences added up to 46 years. Big Bill, as he was known, had not long been released from prison after an explosive bungle. He'd stored sodium chlorate in the Apprentice Boys of Derry Hall in Bridgeton but made the mistake of putting the package next to the oven. When someone put some pies in the oven and lit the gas, the place was blown to smithereens. When police discovered who blew up all the pies, Campbell was jailed for eight years and, by choice, served his sentence in Belfast. After his conviction at the pub bombing trial, he defiantly shouted at one of the cops who'd arrested him, 'Hard luck!', indicating he thought the police were expecting him to get a longer stretch.

Describing the convicted nine as 'wicked, brutal and senseless', Lord Ross said, 'The evidence of this trial has revealed an appalling picture of a gang of thugs intent on obtaining arms and explosives to be sent to Northern Ireland to assist other violent men. In addition, explosives have not only been accumulated in Scotland but put to use here. Those who commit such offences can expect no mercy.'

Interestingly, the trial put the spotlight on an unusual, ancient quirk of Scots Law. The jury had been locked up for hours without food or water as was required by the rules – drawn up 400 years before. Their deliberations took a record 10 hours and 40 minutes and resulted in calls for the repeal of the Act of 1587, which required a verdict before they could leave the jury room. The defence lawyers claimed the rules could have encouraged the jury to rush to a verdict to escape the confines of the room.

It was certainly a shock to find myself at a terrorist bomb blast in Glasgow and, thankfully, wasn't something I encountered again in my career.

The one thing about Glasgow-based travelling professional shoplifters is that they know how to enjoy themselves. One of the gangs we were keeping tabs on planned a celebratory dance after a series of raids, but me and my cop colleagues were determined to be party-poopers. In the late 1970s, this group of thieves proved hard to follow, mainly because they used more than one vehicle and went in convoy. So we concentrated on having an informant who had an intimate knowledge of the gang.

Our tout told us the band of shoplifters were planning a big bash to celebrate the end of a criminal tour, which was to take them in their hired cars from Glasgow north to Auchterarder, Perth, Dundee, Inverness and several unfortunate small towns along the way. They'd picked out a nice hotel in the north of Scotland for their hoolie.

The two men and two women were well known to us. They specialised in the best gear. Expensive clothing such as cashmere and silk and all the sought-after designer labels – only the finest was good enough for them. They had arranged for the resetter, who bought the stolen goods, to meet them at their party hotel and pay cash for their rich pickings. She would arrive in a van driven by her partner and shift all the stolen gear from the hire cars.

A clever move, as the van had not been used in any crime and was not on the police radar. The shoplifters knew they could have been spotted getting into the cars after their thefts or recognised by store security guards, so the transfer also meant they would be clean if they were picked up. They could drive home over 100 miles back to Glasgow after a fruitful trip without having to worry about getting rid of the stuff or getting caught with it.

We heard the resetter would join the thieves at the hotel for drinks and a dance before staying overnight. I was also planning an overnight stay in the Highlands with a group of fellow Scottish Crime Squad detectives. First, I contacted Northern Constabulary to let them know we'd be on their patch. I arranged to meet their CID to inform them of our tout's information. The two hire cars would arrive in their area at about 6pm from the north at the same time as the fence's van arrived from Glasgow. All the stolen goods would be locked in the van for safekeeping, then the six of them would stay in the hotel before heading for Glasgow in the morning.

Our plans were different, but just as clear. We staked out the hotel car park and watched the two cars arrive on cue. After the gear was transferred, we pounced and soon had all six in the local nick – much to their surprise. All the stolen clothing was traced to where it had come from and was eventually valued at several thousand pounds.

The crooks missed their big dance and relaxed hotel break. Our squad checked in to the lovely surroundings of the Cairngorm Hotel in Aviemore, near the thieves' proposed overnight accommodation. We celebrated on their behalf.

My wife loved going shopping in town but I hated it. I could see crime all around me that was invisible to regular customers.

Shoplifters were always on the go and I could spot them a mile off. Some of them I knew by sight, others were obvious to me by the way they acted. It got so bad that I convinced my wife we should do our shopping in Hamilton to get away from the light-fingered Glasgow mob.

But it was even worse there. The filching was rife although I didn't recognise any of the crooks. My better-half told me she didn't know what I was going on about so I subtly directed her to watch various criminals at work. In a short spell we witnessed five thefts in progress.

Back in Glasgow one day in 1979, I was in Marks & Spencer in Trongate, holding my three-month-old daughter in my arms. I was waiting at the exit when I saw two women who were top shoplifters. They were renowned for their skills at pinching from stores and, chillingly, one of them was also well known for having been an accomplished abortionist. They each had two bags, no doubt full of stolen gear. When they saw me they both did an about-turn and then went into a huddle as they discussed what to do about me standing at the door.

Then they strolled up and one of them said, 'Is that your wee wean, Mr McLaughlin?' When I told them it was, she pressed a 50 pence piece into my hand and explained, 'That's for the little one.' It was a nice distraction technique. Before I knew what was happening they'd bustled past me with their bags. I was amazed at their brass neck. Accepting the 50p was the only 'corruption' I was ever involved in!

Shoplifters were like other crooks in their desire to beat security measures. When tags on clothing were brought in it caused the neds problems. The tags set off alarms at the doors of the shop if they hadn't been removed. But there was a way around it for those who went nicking in stores that sold food as well as clothing and other goods.

Wandering into the frozen food section, the shoplifters would pick up a freezer bag and head to the clothing area. They'd stuff their pinched gear into the freezer bag and wander coolly through the alarms at the door. It wouldn't go off because something in the freezer bags blocked the signal from the tags to detectors. The chilled-out crooks had a field day before that scam was discovered.

Criminals can be incredibly sneaky about how they hide their loot. Sometimes we got a tip off from a tout about where money or jewellery was stashed. But we had to be careful when raiding a place to make it look like we'd come across the items by thorough searching rather than because we knew where to look from the start. That way the informant was protected from reprisals.

It could be difficult to pull that off if the hiding place was particularly inventive. One crook put jewels behind his light switches. Another classic we encountered was the thief who hid his stash under stones at the bottom of a large fish tank. Try telling a crook you'd worked that out by chance.

One woman kept her stolen baubles in the tumble drier, wrapped in towels and clothes to protect them. Every time the cops came for an unscheduled visit the drier was rumbling round. But eventually some of the jewellery fell out of the clothing and started ratting loudly in the drum. We soon twigged what was going on and recovered the stuff.

One top getaway driver had stolen gold sovereigns in his house. My information was that he had pulled the head off a teddy bear and concealed the coins among the soft toy's stuffing. I had to search the house and check Ted's tummy without the crook noticing that we knew where to look. We distracted him and a cop grabbed the bear and took it away, squeezing it to ensure the coins were inside. Luckily it wasn't a talking Ted that spoke when it was cuddled or it might have given the game away.

The valuable bear was replaced subtly and we told the man we were planning to bring in a metal detector to go over the house to find the stolen money. He burst, as we say, and spilled his guts – and the contents of the bear's. He pointed us to the toy and we feigned surprised as its head came off and Ted coughed up the coins.

Under the floorboards was always a good place to look, as was up the chimney. One woman had a more unusual place to conceal her stolen rings – in teacups hanging on hooks in her kitchen.

One of the most memorable and satisfying cases involved the theft of cash from a business that was continually broken into. A local woman was doing an impression of Fagin from *Oliver Twist* and sending her young children into the place to pinch the money. They got into the office through a small window that no adult could have squeezed through. We had no prints but we did find a big clue – the name of one of the kids. He'd spotted a typewriter while he was on the rob and had decided to have a shot. The only thing the 11-year-old could think to type was his full name! Thanks very much. We knew who was behind it but we needed proof. So we left five marked pound notes and waited for them to be thieved.

But when we went looking for the money in the crooked mother's house we just couldn't find it. After a couple of visits I was getting very frustrated because we were convinced she was behind it. Later it clicked with me. Each time we'd left empty handed, the smirking woman had offered us a parting gift – a chocolate. 'Would you like a sweetie, officer?' she'd smiled as she'd proffered her box of chocs. We'd thought she was just celebrating outfoxing us. But now I wondered if there was more to it.

I called her and said I was coming back. She wasn't bothered because she took great delight in outsmarting me and, as I was leaving, once again produced her chocolate box. I showed her I didn't have a soft centre when I made my move. I lifted out the layers of chocs and found five £1 notes – the marked money we were looking for. It wiped the smile off her face and was a sweet moment for me because I knew she'd really enjoyed getting one over on us. And all because the lady loved Milk Tray!

14

A KIDNAP MYSTERY, A VOICE FROM THE GRAVE AND THE IRISHMAN

We were thrown into a web of intrigue around 1980 amid a kidnap puzzle. An unexpected call came in from the Metropolitan Police in London, letting us know a squad of their men were on the way to Glasgow on the next flight up. They were surveillance experts, hunting an alleged kidnapper.

The scheming villain had ordered them to Glasgow to await a phone call with vital instructions. In what sounded like the plot of a thriller, the controlling crook had already had the Met officers dashing about London, picking up calls in phone boxes and other locations. Each time he'd told them he wanted cash but would be on the lookout for officers snooping about and wouldn't collect it if he had any fears he was being watched. No doubt a botched pick-up would have put his kidnap victim's life in danger.

The last call from the mystery criminal instructed the London cops to travel to Glasgow and await further instructions. He promised he'd call them at the Albany Hotel, a top venue in the city centre. They needed the help of the Scottish Crime Squad to catch the potentially dangerous mastermind but they were reluctant to tell us much about the supposed kidnapping. Was it a high-profile businessman or a celebrity? They wouldn't give anything away.

In an unlikely twist, the kidnapper had called ahead to reserve rooms for the detectives from the Smoke. Of course, he hadn't paid in advance for the accommodation. The Met boys didn't stay in the pre-booked rooms. They also reserved rooms next door to likely characters who had booked in to the hotel that day and could be the kidnapper keeping an eye on them.

We offered to help with monitoring these other guests but they insisted they had the latest hi-tech surveillance equipment at their disposal. The Met got those things first so we took them at their word. But I later walked into one of the rooms and found one of the London cops listening in to the activities next door in an old-fashioned way – he had his ear pressed to a glass against the wall. Our visitors had forgotten their snooping gear in the rush to fly north.

The kidnapper's call was made to the hotel and a series of other phone messages followed as he sent the police around and about all day. The last call said he would phone an Ayrshire pub that evening with the final instructions. The Met squad were exhausted after 24 hours on the go so we became fully operational to help them.

I was in the pub when the call came in. The crook had said he would phone and ask for 'George' so we were ready when the barmaid called out that name and indicated the phone. The last set of orders was bizarre. The kidnapper growled his instructions in minute detail. He wanted a ransom of £100,000 – about £300,000 at today's prices. We were to place used notes in a large plastic barrel and throw it in the water tied by a rope to the end of the derelict Fairlie Pier in Ayrshire.

At the run-down pier we found the barrel waiting for us, a strong rope attached to it. We didn't have £100,000 handy so we cut up pieces of paper to note size and stuffed them in the container. That was topped off with £100 in marked notes so the bandit would see some real cash when he prized the lid off the barrel. It was tightly sealed up and launched into the water, tethered to the pier by the rope.

All we could do was sit back and watch. As DS, my job was to gather a team to keep an eye on the entrance to the pier to ensure no one got near the floating ransom. We had officers posted nearby, ready to rush in if we had to make an arrest.

We settled down in our surveillance van, which kept us cosy during the mid-winter night. There was snow on the ground which meant we could keep an eye out for fresh footprints at the scene. But the hours passed with no sign of anyone going near the pier. Was our kidnapper playing more games?

Feeling rested, the Met team arrived to take over early next morning and I went for a stroll to the end of the pier with one of their cops. We both stood open-mouthed when we looked into the water. There was the rope – cut through. The barrel was gone! I was astonished. There had been no boats approaching the site overnight. We'd been stung and came to the conclusion that a diver must have braved the icy conditions to swim up under cover of darkness and grab his booty. It was James Bond stuff, indeed. It was a pity we couldn't have kept an eyeball on the barrel but he'd made sure that was impossible thanks to its location.

Trouble was, the kidnapper knew he had been given £100 instead of £100,000. What would that mean for his victim, whoever they were? Well, we never found out. There were no more phone calls from the mastermind and the Met did not tell us what the outcome was. The media didn't carry any stories about a kidnapping or a victim being hurt or killed because of a failed ransom pick-up.

All very mysterious and rumours abounded in our squad about the whole operation. A favourite theory was that it had been set up by one of the security services as a test to see how the police in England and Scotland would cope with a high-profile kidnapping. I doubt we'll ever know the truth.

I'm fascinated by cases that are legal firsts. Like the incredible time a 'voice from the grave' helped me snare a killer in a baffling missing body case. Murderer Michael Topham confessed after believing he was being taunted by his victim – over the radio.

The chilling case made legal history in 1980 when Topham admitted murder even though the body of John Coughlan, who'd been missing for five years, was never found. Just like the later case of murdered Edinburgh woman Suzanne Pilley in 2010, police searched a forest for a grave. And just as the cops failed to find Ms Pilley's remains in Argyll, they didn't recover John Coughlan's body from the site near the Queen's Balmoral estate.

There had been at least one previous murder trial in Scotland where a killer was found guilty without a body. But this case was a legal landmark because Topham actually pled guilty despite his victim never being found.

It certainly was a strange series of events that led to Topham, then 35, being sentenced to life at the High Court in Glasgow on September 8, 1980.

The squad was investigating a series of housebreakings in Glasgow's Southside. The locals in Pollokshaws and surrounding areas were being targeted for their jewellery in a string of afternoon break-ins. We 'looked up' some well-kent faces in the area but had no luck. After several days around there, myself and a colleague spotted a likely character. The youth was acting suspiciously, toting a heavy bag, and lurking about as if he was waiting for somebody. Thinking the bag could be full of house-breaking kit, we pounced.

Leaping from our unmarked car, we nabbed him. The bag had no tools in it. But even better – it was full of jewellery! Thinking we'd hit the jackpot, we took the lad to the station for questioning. He denied any link to the Southside jewellery thefts. A bit of checking confirmed he was telling the truth. The baubles didn't match anything on our list of stolen trinkets. It later turned out they'd been pinched from somewhere in the north of the city and our boy had been hanging about waiting for a well-known resetter – better known as a 'fence' – to meet him and pick up the jewels.

The youth was unfamiliar with being quizzed by cops and evidently thought we were planning to charge him with the Southside raids. Of course, we weren't, but he felt it was in his interest to try to do some bargaining. He said his father had told him he knew how the police 'worked'. Dad had advised junior that, if he were ever in trouble with the cops, he should offer up some information that would help them crack some other crimes and put him in the good books.

I jokingly told him he'd have to solve a murder or another equally serious crime before any 'deal' would be considered. To the astonishment of me and my colleague, he said he could do just that! He then went on to give us details of a murder – a crime we didn't even know had happened.

He told us he'd been working with Michael Topham, who was a tradesman. Topham had been listening to music on the radio before a programme about séances and the afterlife came on. The presenter claimed to have recorded voices from beyond the grave and they hissed from the tranny. Topham was suddenly so shocked he fell off the trellis he'd been standing on. He broke down and confessed to the colleague he thought he'd heard the voice of a man he'd murdered!

The story sounded like a fantasy. Surely the lad was trying to stall for time? He was unable to name the dead man and we had no date for the alleged murder. More puzzling still, there were no outstanding deaths on the books that matched the details of the unlikely tale.

Our informant had given us sufficient information to track down the flat where the tradesmen had supposedly been working when the mysterious killing took place. The homeowner, unaware we were trying to prove his flat was a murder scene, gave us the name of the contractor. From there we got a list of employees. We discovered that one of the men hadn't been seen or heard of – for five years! Now our noses were twitching.

John Coughlan, a family man from Blantyre, had left home for work in June 1975 and never returned. His wife had reported him missing but the cops had drawn a blank. So he was officially a missing person, not a murder victim. We searched the flat where he'd been working and were amazed to discover old bloodstains soaked into the floorboards. We looked up Mr Coughlan's blood group on his missing persons file. It was a match.

Michael Topham was taken to the station and I quizzed him. He was calm and compliant but became aggressive any time I got near the horrible truth. After a tough stand-off he finally admitted he'd killed his victim with a hammer and a window weight, taken from a sash window he was replacing. He'd brutally battered to death Mr Coughlan, who was 57. He was a caretaker who was looking after the properties while they were being renovated and had caught Topham stealing paint.

After his murderous assault, Topham had fled to his elderly grandmother's house in Aberdeenshire. There, submerged in a septic tank, we found a lead weight similar to the murder weapon. But where was the missing man? Topham said he'd buried Mr Coughlan in Alltcailleach Forest by the A93 between Braemar and Crathie, a road known as the Miler. But a massive search by cops, using sniffer dogs and even a military thermal scanner, couldn't locate the lonely grave.

I charged Topham and another man, who was alleged to have helped him move the body. Topham made his historic admission in court while his co-accused had his plea of not guilty accepted. Topham was released from prison in 1991 and died eight years later. Nearly four decades after the murder, the location of John Coughlan's grave remains a mystery.

One of the most memorable Glasgow crime lords was Irishman John Friel. I first heard of Friel in the late 1970s when he was released from prison after a stretch for being caught with a gun and explosives in a Glasgow club. He was given seven years for possessing the gelignite and another year, to run concurrently, for having the revolver. The crime was said to have had sectarian overtones and Friel was refused bail before the 1971 trial because the Crown claimed he had IRA links. The court case was held amid tight security, with uniformed and plainclothes officers on guard.

Born in Donegal in 1944, Friel was a master of the blarney but his gift of the gab never extended to spilling the beans on criminal pursuits. After several meetings with him, I quickly realised he would talk for ages and tell you nothing you wanted to hear.

He masterminded a series of fraudulent schemes from which he made vast fortunes. One of them was called 'the lump' and involved him claiming to have supplied Irish workers to the building trade through a government scheme. But he didn't provide all of the men he claimed for and civil servants were forever chasing him to recover cash he'd fraudulently obtained from them.

Flamboyant bar owner Friel attracted attention by driving around Glasgow in a Rolls-Royce. A neat trick, considering he only ever had a provisional licence. He had the private registration number JF1 on the Rolls. Of course, it wasn't the genuine article. That would have cost him thousands to buy from the vehicle licensing people. The fancy plate impressed certain folk so he took the risk of being caught and prosecuted for having it on his car. Friel – or 'Free-ell', as he liked to be known among posh circles – was happy to take the fine because it cost him a lot less than buying the real plate.

The amiable Irishman built up an empire of property, mainly hotels, restaurants and pubs, and had plenty of associates in the criminal fraternity and also in high places.

I arrested Friel in 1980 after getting a warrant for him and three others who'd formed a fraudulent scheme to get hold of bottles of spirits worth over £28,000. We had to get into the bank account of the company they used for the crooked con so we obtained a second warrant to authorise access to the books of an Irish bank to study the firm's dealings and Friel's transactions. He was convicted and sentenced to six months. The law wasn't finished with him and he was in trouble again in 1985 when he was jailed for a year and fined £7,500 after being charged with travelling to London to buy cocaine.

Despite his dangerous lifestyle, and a showdown with another top crook that I describe later in this book, Friel lived into his sixties and died of natural causes in 2009. He was said to have had a heart attack, following a previous stroke. According to reports, the Irish crime boss died leaving debts of £1.5 million on his property empire.

15

THE BODY IN THE BONFIRE AND THE TARTAN TERRORIST

Being a taxi driver can be a dangerous job – even more so if you're a woman. There was shock in October 1982 when the body of cabbie Cathy McChord was found stuffed into her taxi's luggage compartment in a quiet cul-de-sac in Cambuslang. She'd been stabbed in the back of the head, in the neck and three times in the chest. Residents found the vehicle with the meter still ticking over and called the police about their suspicions.

I was now back in the Serious Crime Squad and my colleagues were puzzling over the killing. Was it the work of a crazed stranger or could it be linked to 36-year-old Mrs McChord's colourful criminal past? She'd been a key player in a dramatic £143,000 newspaper 'spot-the-ball' competition fraud five years before and had been jailed for the con. Her devious scheme was only stopped after one of the bogus winners had blown the lid off it to one of my squad colleagues.

Teenager James McCreadie had feared for his life after being allegedly threatened by heavies that he'd be 'chucked in the Clyde with a concrete overcoat' because he hadn't paid the fraud organisers their share of the crooked competition winnings. Mr McCreadie was one of nearly 70 people who'd 'won' the rigged 'Place The Ball' contest in the *Scottish Daily Express*. The competition involved trying to guess where the ball had been before it was removed from a photo taken during a football match.

Cathy McChord and a colleague, who both worked in the newspaper department that ran the competition, had arranged for people to win the £1,500 prize then give her and her gang a £1,300 kickback. But 19-year-old Mr McCreadie had blown most of his winnings by the time the crooks had come for their share and could only give them £600. Fearing reprisals, he'd spilled his guts to police.

It had then emerged that Mrs McChord had craved more money than her £35-a-week job in the competitions department could give her. Desperate to escape her tenement home in Baillieston, she had scooped around £17,000 by taking a £500 cut from each of the bogus £1,500 winners. Twice she'd also rigged jackpots of over £20,000, pocketing a third. She'd put £12,000 in building society accounts and bought a luxurious £18,000 home in the suburbs, with expensive fittings and décor. She'd also treated her taxi driver husband Eddie to a new cab and herself to a £3,500 car, expensive clothes from London's best shops and gone on lavish holidays with her husband.

Mrs McChord and her cohorts had pled guilty to the fraud, avoiding the need for a trial with 70 witnesses. She'd been jailed for three years. But there was no legislation in place at that time to recover the proceeds of crime and only £4,000 of the £143,000 in ill-gotten gains was ever found by the police. Speaking later to the press, Mrs McChord had explained, 'I enjoy spending money. I like good things – wine, food, travel. And I love clothes, particularly trouser suits. I did make flights to London to buy clothes. Whenever I had money from the competitions, I would take it to two building societies. I would put between £100 and £300 in one and about the same amount in the other.'

Now she was dead. Could the enemies she'd made through her fraud be behind it? The team continued to investigate but then they were stunned by the second murder of a woman in Cambuslang in two months.

In December, 48-year-old nurse Elizabeth Walton was hurrying home from the local train station late at night when she was pounced upon and knocked unconscious. She was stripped and strangled and, in a macabre ceremony, the killer carved symbolic and ritualistic knife wounds after death.

I was brought in to help probe that case. Three days after the murder a man arrived at the police caravan at the scene. Iain Scoular claimed he'd seen a suspicious stranger near the railway embankment where the victim had been found. But the 24-year-old, something of an oddball who still lived with his parents, only succeeded in putting himself in the frame. He was interviewed ten times and changed his story about his movements on the night of the killing.

His overprotective mother complained to cops about the repeated interest in her son but she inadvertently dropped him in it. She said she'd waited up for him to come home on the night of the murder and had gone out in the car looking for him, finally spotting him after 1am. That contrasted with forklift truck driver Scoular's story that he'd been back home just after 11pm.

Among key forensic evidence linking Scoular to the victim was the ligature used to strangle Mrs Walton. It was similar to the draw-cord from the anorak Scoular wore at work. The cord from Scoular's jacket was missing and his explanations were unsatisfactory. Forensic experts trawled shops and markets to find clothing with similar cords but discovered nothing. Scoular's trousers also had musk rat hair on them. The victim's coat was made from musk rat pelt.

Now the net was closing in on Scoular. But could the same man be responsible for the other Cambuslang killing – the knife murder of Cathy McChord? Officers found there seemed to be something ritualistic about the killing, like Mrs Walton's death. Everyday objects like her cigarettes, lighter, asthma inhaler and other items had been carefully arranged in a row in the taxi.

Witnesses also identified Scoular as a man seen running from the vehicle.

Scoular was eventually charged with both crimes and appeared in court in June 1983, claiming a special defence of alibi. Said to be of low intelligence, Scoular seemed unperturbed by the trial and laughed and joked with police officers. The jury heard he was sexually inadequate but Strathclyde Police's chief medical officer Dr William McLay said there was a 'perverse sexual motivation' to the way Mrs Walton's body had been 'decorated' with knife wounds. The accused was said to be an extremely dangerous psychopath. To the horror of his tearful fiancée, who was in the court, the jury found him guilty by a majority of stabbing Mrs McChord and convicted him unanimously of Mrs Walton's murder. He was given two life sentences with a minimum of 20 years and was released in 2003.

The discovery of dead bodies in unusual situations was something that came up throughout my career. Few were as gruesome as the tale of the body that was put on a Bonfire Night pyre in a bid to dispose of the evidence of the crime. I was called to investigate at the start of 1983. At a house in Pollok, cleansing workers had made the shocking discovery of human remains in the remnants of a bonfire that had been blazing around the time of Guy Fawkes Night, nine weeks before.

A council worker called to the unoccupied home had been traumatised by the discovery of a woman's head in the burnt-out bonfire. The 19-year-old lad and his colleague had been sent to clear out the house, which was stripped of furniture and only had a fridge and washing machine in it. Unfortunately for them, they'd also been tasked with tidying up the garden. As they'd used their rakes to sort through the debris, they'd made the grim find. The victim's charred body was also in the shocking home-made cremation fire.

Our forensic experts scoured the remnants of the twisted scene. They discovered bloodstains on floorboards in the bedroom. There was also evidence that an attempt had been made to set fire to the house.

We spoke to neighbours, as the previous tenant of the home was obviously in our sights as a suspect. They told us they remembered the fifth of November and the days surrounding it. They'd seen the neighbour, Edward Duncan, stoking the blaze around Bonfire Night.

One neighbour said she'd heard someone cry out, 'Mammy!' around the time of the incident and had seen Duncan next morning, standing beside the blaze and loading furniture on to it. He was, according to witnesses, spotted feeding the fire by chucking more furniture on to it, sometimes out of his bedroom window. Unusually, he took a close interest in how it was burning – for a couple of days after the end of the traditional bonfire season. Eventually, we were told, the fire brigade had turned up to douse the flames, unaware of the horror among the burned furniture.

We went looking for Duncan. He saw publicity about the horrific crime and gave himself up. He was interviewed by the senior divisional detective officer, who contacted the Serious Crime Squad so we could get a voluntary statement, outlining the tragic events of the previous November 5. I took the statement.

The victim, we had discovered, was Jean Miller, a 50-year-old woman Duncan had met while out on the town. Duncan, who was 34, had arrived back home with Mrs Miller, a tiny woman of 4ft 10ins. Duncan seemed remorseful and keen to cooperate. He was emotional as he laid out the events of the night and signed his voluntary statement.

He told me that he had been unable to perform sexually that night and she had mocked him over it. In a rage he had hit her, later realising that she was dead. Panicking, he had taken advantage of the fact that it was bonfire time. He'd wrapped her lifeless body in a carpet and carried her downstairs and outside to dispose of her in his makeshift funeral pyre.

No doubt fearing his punishment, he went to the shockingly extreme lengths instead of calling for help. He was charged with Mrs Miller's murder. Surely, after that confession, it was an open and shut case?

But you can't beat a clever lawyer. Duncan employed redoubtable QC Nicholas Fairbairn, who insisted to the court that his client should not be convicted of murder. He said there was insufficient evidence, given the course of events.

Experts had been unable to determine an exact cause of death from Mrs Miller's charred remains. Her skull showed no fractures despite the fact she was punched by Duncan. There was a possibility that the frail victim had choked on her own blood after being hit while in Duncan's bedroom.

There was legal debate after the jury was sent out. When they returned the judge, Lord Robertson, told them there had been a 'speedy development' and legal submissions by the defence and the Crown had convinced him there was no case to answer for murder.

Mr Fairbairn said his client, who did not give evidence, would plead guilty to assaulting his victim by punching her on the head. It may seem unusual, but that was the law, despite the horror of the bonfire disposal attempt. After all, Mrs Miller was dead before her body was put into the flames.

Duncan got six months for the bizarre crime. After the trial at the High Court in Glasgow, he spent only about one more week in jail as he'd already been in prison for a while on remand. Compared to murder, an assault conviction was probably a shock to the victim's family. During the trial her husband revealed they had two children and had separated a year before. He said she'd had a drink problem and the last he'd heard of her she'd been living in a hostel.

At least she was finally given a proper funeral after the horror of Duncan's bizarre cremation bid.

'Have clipboard, will travel' was an unofficial motto of the boys in the Serious Crime Squad. When the team was sent out of Glasgow on a murder case it was clear we would be there until the crime was solved. That could take weeks, running up a big overtime bill for the force, which was some consolation to our hard-working troops, who had to shuttle back and forth to our base.

But I wasn't flavour of the month with some of my squad colleagues when we went on a big job in Renfrewshire – and I cracked the case within three hours. The lads who'd been preparing themselves for another long haul, and the extra pay that went with it, were surprised to find themselves heading back to Glasgow on the same day they'd arrived.

It was June 1983 and a body had been found in the water in the seaside town of Gourock. It looked like foul play so me and my colleagues in the heavy mob were soon in town. The boss called us together for a 10am briefing. He told us the victim, George West, was a popular local character, who'd worked as an unofficial porter for local taxi drivers. He was 34 but had a mental age of ten. Family had revealed he'd been having a hard time from local youths. They'd been hassling him so much George and his mother had planned to leave town to get away from the troublemakers.

All the detectives were given the names and addresses of youths who were worth checking out. We needed to know where they'd been on the night George died, below the local pier, after being struck with something and left for dead by the water.

One of the first doors I knocked on belonged to 17-year-old David Anderson. As my colleague and I entered his home, he appeared nervous. When we began to question him he made a strange request. Could his girlfriend come to the house as he needed to speak to her urgently? He said it would be worth our while if we agreed. My suspicions were piqued and I said she could be present, as long as I was there too.

When she arrived he stunned us all by making a full confession to her. He was emotional at having to break the news but he wanted her to be the first to know. She was very tearful on hearing what he had to say. I looked at my colleague in amazement. It was barely three hours since we'd started on the case. Now we were taking our suspect to the local police station.

The story that unfolded about George's death was as tragic as all the others. Wearing his trademark cab driver's peaked cap, he'd earned cash from tips given to him for carrying ferry passengers' luggage to local taxis. He'd kept a book with a list of his meagre earnings. Taxi drivers would pencil in a note of the tips they'd given him because he couldn't read or write. He'd also handed out cards with taxi numbers to help the drivers.

Touchingly, he'd been saving up his cash for a holiday to Blackpool with his mum. It was thought in the early stages of the inquiry that the cabbies may have clubbed together to give him a holiday bonus and he could have been killed for that money. It was a measure of George's 'mental handicap', as it was called then, that he couldn't operate the fruit machines at the local arcade and needed help to play them, according to one witness.

When he was reported missing at 11pm, the taxi drivers he worked with carried out a desperate all-night search. One of them was unfortunate enough to find him in the water at around 4am, his injured body clad in orange waterproof trousers and an anorak.

The murder had taken place minutes after our suspect David Anderson had downed ten pints at the railway station bar with his pals. As they'd strolled to the chip shop around 10pm, he'd disappeared off to find somewhere to pee. But one of his mates claimed he'd reappeared in a panic. The friend had grabbed Anderson as he'd sprinted past the chippie. 'I've just weighed in

George. I think I've killed him,' Anderson was alleged to have said. It later emerged that the teenager had been seen running from the pier around the time of the crime. Another witness claimed he'd confessed to him, too, blurting out, 'I've just given George a doing. I think I've killed him. I think he's dead.'

At his trial at the High Court in Glasgow that September, Anderson denied striking George with a plank of wood and leaving him unconscious and severely injured below the high-water level. He didn't give evidence but his QC said George had made an 'improper' suggestion to Anderson when they'd met under the pier. However, George's doctor told the court his patient had a condition that rendered him sexually harmless. By a majority, the jury found Anderson guilty of murder and he was ordered to be detained without limit of time.

We'd arrived at the murder scene without a time limit, too, but my break in finding the killer so quickly produced a great result and saved the force a fortune in overtime.

The fight for Scottish independence wasn't always a peaceful, political one. In the 1980s, Special Branch was keeping tabs on radical and potentially violent separatist groups such as the Scottish National Liberation Army. I was a DS in the Serious Crime Squad in 1983 when I was asked by Special Branch colleagues to assist in a covert surveillance operation of a suspect feared to be planning letter bomb attacks on prominent figures.

The cops had an informant inside the world of the extremist groups. Bernard Goodwin was feeding them information about the actions and movements of suspected 'tartan terrorist' Thomas Kelly. The 28-year-old shipyard worker was feared to be a bomb-maker. Mr Goodwin, a psychiatric nurse, was a 24-year-old former police cadet who'd agreed to work with cops after becoming alarmed by the increasing 'clandestine cloak-and-dagger activities' he claimed were being planned by members of groups he was connected with, including one called Seed of the Gael.

He informed detectives he'd been told by one member that the group planned to mount raids by sea on top-secret naval bases on the Clyde coast at Ardentinny and Coulport and send letter bombs to high-profile people, including Trade Secretary Norman Tebbit.

I was among the team who tailed Kelly at one point. He was definitely aware of police surveillance procedures and took various measures to avoid being followed. He'd change buses regularly and even try to confuse us by jumping off a bus at the same time as someone who looked similar to him.

Special Branch also asked me to visit another man allegedly linked to the Scottish National Liberation Army. They had raided his place so many times he knew their procedure so they needed a new face to check up on him. They probably also wanted to avoid a complaint about their regular visits.

He was not your typical image of a 'terrorist', quite charming as he sat in his home, surrounded by shelves of books. My inquiries with my sources suggested he did want Scotland to be separate but it was debatable whether he agreed with the SNLA's violent aims.

However, the focus was still on Kelly. Special Branch had bugged Mr Goodwin's house, putting a microphone under the floorboards, and recorded conversations between him and Kelly. Mr Goodwin claimed Kelly had asked him how to spell 'bomb' while he was writing a letter. The tout also told the cops that Kelly had nearly blown himself up in September 1983 while building a bomb in the bedroom of the house.

The device had flared up and glowed orange, Mr Goodwin recalled, before Kelly had thrown it into the corner of the room as smoke poured from it. The carpet was burned but, obviously, the fire brigade wasn't called. Next day Kelly built another bomb and the pair set out from Mr Goodwin's

Drumchapel home, tailed by Special Branch, who'd been poised outside.

According to Mr Goodwin, the sly Kelly lost his pursuers by cutting across some waste ground and the pair got into a taxi with the bomb, arriving in the city to post it. Mr Goodwin said he watched in horror as Kelly forced the package into the slot of a post box in Ingram Street. They went to a pub in London Road and Kelly sneaked out and informed a Special Branch officer outside where the bomb was. Later, dozens of cops burst in and arrested them.

The explosive device, addressed to Norman Tebbit, was checked out by bomb disposal experts and declared capable of causing serious injury.

At Kelly's trial at the High Court in Glasgow in January 1984 there was heavy police security and members of separatist groups packed the public benches to see Mr Goodwin – Scotland's first 'supergrass' – betray his former cohorts. Kelly eventually changed his plea to guilty. He admitted making the explosive that blew up in the house and the device posted to Mr Tebbit. The Crown accepted his pleas of not guilty to conspiring with others at various houses and bars in Glasgow to send explosives by post to prominent public figures and institutions in the UK, and a fraud charge. His counsel said the accused had carried out the offences at his own instigation and the letter bomb had been intended to focus attention on the Scottish cause. Kelly was jailed for ten years.

The QC had tried to undermine Mr Goodwin as a witness by suggesting he'd never left the police and had been on the Special Branch payroll. But Mr Goodwin stood up to the tough questioning, insisting he'd been paid only travel expenses of £100 during the three-month operation. He said he'd tried to drop out of the groups but was chillingly told that, having become a member of Seed of the Gael, he could never leave. Encouraged by police to stay in touch with the extremists, he was elected to the high council of the Scottish Republican Socialist Party, he said. He claimed that he discovered the SRSP had links with the SNLA and it worked on the same basis as the IRA and Sinn Fein.

The prosecutor, William Nimmo-Smith QC, praised Mr Goodwin for his bravery in giving evidence and said it remained to be seen what risks might affect his future. Mr Goodwin was put under police protection and newspapers agreed to a request from Strathclyde Police top brass not to publish his photograph. Threats to Mr Goodwin were said to have come from Irish sources, possibly the Irish National Liberation Army.

Interestingly, convicted tartan terrorist Thomas Kelly reverted to the legal independence fight after he got out of jail in 1990. Kelly joined the Scottish National Party a year after his release and became local party secretary. He assisted during the council election campaign after being rejected as a local candidate by the SNP's vetting committee. In 1995 he was acting as an SNP election agent and admitted his shame about his past. He described himself as 'very angry and a bit daft' when he committed his crimes and said it had been 'pointless and stupid', adding he regretted it.

16

SMOOTHIE SUSIE AND THE HEIST EXTRADITION

The big crimes like murder, rape and robbery often stick in the minds of police officers. But I always felt the lesser offences that didn't get the same publicity could cause a great deal of trauma. To my mind, housebreaking was a crime that was 'under-rated' by the justice system. Anyone who intrudes on someone's personal space and steals from them should automatically be dealt with in a higher court.

I lost count of the number of times I went to a victim's house and found the owner distraught. They often said they felt personally violated and didn't want to stay in their home any more. Many elderly women were specifically targeted because they had all their jewellery in a box, which meant they lost the lot when a sticky-fingered raider appeared.

The trinkets had great sentimental value even though their value as scrap gold was low and they'd been bought decades before at a small price. But they were family heirlooms – priceless.

Some of the thieves I encountered specialised in entering homes, not by stealth, but by deception – an equally despicable crime. Over the years, one of those characters particularly stood out. They called her Smoothie Susie. She was a bogus caller who conned her way around town and beyond. Her nickname came from the press, much like other eye-catching tags such as Bible John.

171

She'd knock the door of elderly folk, mainly women, and tell them she was there to help them. She posed as a social worker, home help, council employee, member of the Department of Health and Social Security or another role that won the trust of her aged victim.

Her foot in the door, she'd chat nicely to the householder, using her skills to give her an air of authority and knowledge of caring. Her prey would relax and trust her. Some were pretty much housebound and she even went so far as to make sure one woman got safely into bed and others were tucked in before she waved them a cheery goodbye.

All the folk she dropped in on, a large number, were satisfied she was a very decent person when she left. It was only some time later the victim would discover her handbag or purse, or both, had been stolen by the unexpected visitor. Or a drawer had been searched for cash.

Smoothie Susie came to my attention in May 1984 when she struck against a 94-year-old woman. Posing as a social work employee, she made off with the victim's purse, bag, pension book and £143 in notes.

Her reign of mayhem dragged on, with folk from their late '60s into their late '90s being hit. The victims were well chosen but we didn't know how she was picking these easy targets. We weren't even sure if the same person was doing the crimes. We only discovered later that she'd change her hair colour every other week. A detective sergeant at Craigie Street Police Office in F Division, where I was based, had been collating all the details of Smoothie Susie's crimes and I was well aware of the case, codenamed Operation Prey. When he retired I eagerly took over the file, determined to crack it.

By October 1985 we had over 30 similar crimes reported in the same area. We tried to flush out Susie with publicity and got some good press and TV coverage. One person helped us produce a photofit likeness of her, which was circulated publicly.

Susie went quiet for a while then popped up in a different patch of Glasgow. Another media blitz, another period of inactivity, then she was back in action, this time in Bearsden. The pattern continued as she kept moving, from the Southside to Partick.

Often the bags and purses would be found discarded. Invariably it was just cash that was taken from them and any credit cards and other property in the bag were left undisturbed. Good people would hand in the abandoned bags. Less salubrious individuals would try to use the pension books and credit cards. We were sidetracked at one point when some stolen cards were used but it turned out the culprit was someone who'd found a purse Susie had chucked away. That took us no further forward.

Eventually we got a break. One elderly woman told us the bogus caller had handled a framed photo. We had our first real clue – fingerprints. But there was no match in the system which suggested our smooth criminal had no previous convictions.

I had by now worked out that Susie probably had a medical background of some type due to her knowledge of the caring system and I went to hospitals in the south of the city, including the Victoria Infirmary. I showed the photofit around but the staff couldn't help.

We even had a large map on the wall, showing where she had struck, in an effort to work out where she might go next. Graphs outlined the pattern of her targets. It was tough work without computers to help. Mapping where we found dumped bags we noted that if she'd been working the southside, the bag was usually abandoned towards the east. If she struck in Partick, the stuff was often dumped in the east as well. So it was more than likely she lived on that side of Glasgow.

Our woman had used the same fake names over and over again. At one point, towards the end of her spate of crimes, she pretended to be a female police officer and, in a bizarre coincidence, gave herself the name of a detective who worked with me at the time.

I reckoned this was a vital clue. It was my theory that people who've had a run-in with the police never forget the officer's name. They even sometimes use the name of a cop they know to add credibility if they're impersonating a police officer.

I spoke to my female colleague, whose name had been misappropriated, and showed her the latest photofit. It reminded her of a woman she'd dealt with some years before, so she searched her old notebooks. Bingo! The case, from 1974, involved a woman who was accused of conning old ladies in the same way and, after a trial, had not been convicted. So her fingerprints weren't on file.

Now we knew Smoothie Susie's real name – Williamina Watson. In her fifties, she was an unlikely candidate for a conwoman. The loving wife and mother-of-three was involved in the health service, as I had suspected. She was a nursing sister in the geriatric unit at Glasgow's Victoria Infirmary, which was near to Craigie Street Police Office.

You'd have thought she'd have had a caring attitude to the elderly but Watson exploited her job. She targeted the pensioners for money, scouring hospital files to find their home addresses. I checked her shift schedule and found she'd been off work every time a crime had been committed.

Operation Prey swung into action to nab her in the act. She was put under surveillance, starting at her home. We had a clue about the car used by Susie. One witness had seen a handbag being thrown from a vehicle by a woman and had picked it up. It belonged to one of the victims. We didn't have a registration number for the car, but we had a make, model and colour. A car parked outside the Watson's home matched Susie's vehicle.

We realised one of the stolen bags had been recovered from a cemetery, near the grave of Watson's mother. More evidence. It wasn't long before she drove off in the car and was seen trying to get into the home of another elderly woman in Rutherglen. She was arrested by the delighted troops.

Watson was charged but, incredibly, she continued to offend while out on bail. Her area of attack increased and she began striking beyond Glasgow, into Largs, Renfrew, Stenhousemuir and Edinburgh. The compulsive con artist was re-arrested. By now the spate of robberies had been continuing for nearly four years. How many of her elderly victims were still alive, I wondered? Sadly, some had died.

We suspected Watson had probably carried out between 350 and 400 Smoothie Susie thefts and she was reported to the procurator fiscal for nearly 90. He proceeded with 33. Williamina Watson was 54 when she appeared in court in July 1988 and she pled guilty to 24 charges of fraud, theft and attempted theft from old folk between September 1984 and March 1988, netting her over £2,700.

The court heard her first victim, an 84-year-old woman, had been stung within ten minutes of the despicable Watson turning up. Posing as a home help, she'd charmed her way into the home of the pensioner, who used a walking stick. Then she'd asked the old lady to hobble to her bedroom window to point out the home of another pensioner Susie claimed to be planning to visit.

When her victim's back was turned, the heartless conwoman had swiped her bag and must have been delighted to rifle through it later and find an astonishing £900 in cash. Her victim had been saving up for a new three-piece suite. One of her oldest targets, a widow of nearly 90, had her life blighted by the 15 minutes it took Susie, posing as a DHSS official, to find her purse, containing £70, and disappear.

Doctors said that they could make no sense of Watson's actions in psychological terms and the court heard the thefts were out of character. Perhaps not, if you'd taken into account the charges she'd faced 14 years before!

The sheriff took pity on her and deferred sentence for a year on the condition Watson attended a psychiatric clinic and repaid her victims. Twelve months on, she was admonished, which didn't strike me as a fair sentence for her crimes.

To my mind, Smoothie Susie showed no remorse and was only in it for the money. I recall she was non-communicative when I quizzed her about her crimes and when I saw her on ID parades. After her trial she told the press she didn't know why she'd done it and she'd spent the money on everyday things. Her husband insisted she was not evil, just in need of help.

I called the hospital and took great delight in telling one of her bosses, who hadn't had the time of the day for me when I'd been there previously and had dismissed my inquiries out of hand. I reminded her of the photofit and told her my suspect had been right under her nose.

But I'll never forget one of the elderly victims, who lived in Partick. I went to see her after we had our suspect. I recall she was over 90 and was very emotional when I spoke to her about the robbery, which had been a couple of years before. She broke down as she explained she wasn't bothered about the money that had been stolen. Her real heartbreak was losing her late husband's wedding ring, which had been in her stolen bag. This news had a big effect on me as I knew the great sentimental value of jewellery to people, especially women.

I was sure the woman we had arrested was responsible and, if true to form, had left the ring in the stolen handbag. I got the date of the robbery and asked the police lost-and-found department to dig out everything they could for the full month. I had previously only asked the department to search for found property up to seven days after each of the spate of crimes.

Knowing it would probably not lead anywhere, I kept my fingers crossed. Luckily, the bag had been handed in two weeks after the robbery and the department had the name and address of the person who'd found it. The ring had been in it but, as no one had claimed it after six months, the finder had been given it to keep. She was a younger woman, who'd held on to the trinket, realising it must have been someone's pride and joy. She happily handed it over to me.

I took the ring to the elderly lady's house and showed her it. Her face lit up as she confirmed it was her husband's ring. That was one of the most rewarding moments I had. Seeing that woman's delighted reaction was worth a million pounds and added to the satisfaction of nabbing the notorious Smoothie Susie.

At one point during the 1980s, an informant had a word in my ear about a notorious criminal who was wanted for a major armed robbery. He was bad news for society so we were eager to get him out of the road as swiftly as possible.

My tipster said our man was driving about in a stolen car with dodgy plates. The motor was a Rover, which was a nice car. The informant kindly gave us the licence number and we went to all the places we knew our target frequented and others we suspected he could turn up in.

But the days passed and we had no luck spotting the car we'd been told to look out for. The sly crook would normally park the car several streets away, we reckoned, to make sure he wasn't anywhere near it if it was found. It was very frustrating because we knew the quicker he was put away the better for the safety of the public.

I was going on holiday and set to head for Australia the next day. With some errands to run, I headed to the East End to go to the shops. I slid my motor into a space just beside a zebra crossing. My messages complete, I left the shop and saw a scene that left me absolutely furious. Some swine had parked on the crossing's zigzag lines and, trying to squeeze in as much as possible, had reversed right up to my car.

He'd blocked me in with no room to manoeuvre. I may have been in holiday mode but you're always a copper, and I knew stopping on those lines was an offence. The driver's terrible parking just added to my bubbling anger.

I took a stroll round the vehicle and gradually my bad mood lifted. It was a Rover! It couldn't be, could it? A check of the licence plate revealed it was the very car I'd been looking for all that time. I knew the number by heart after the continuous searching for it.

Of course, the baddie wasn't in it. But he couldn't be far away. I wasn't going to miss this opportunity. There was a police station just round the corner so I popped in and told the local officers they had a notorious wanted man on their patch, ripe for the picking.

They sprang into action to make sure they nabbed him. I would have liked to have stayed around to witness developments but I had other things to do before jetting off abroad. Luckily, I was able to extricate my car when the vehicle behind me left so I drove off with a satisfied smile and waited for news.

My first day back after my break was brightened by the confirmation from my delighted colleagues that the armed robber had been successfully apprehended after my eagle-eye had tracked him down. He was later jailed. A parking offence that led to a stiffer penalty than normal, I'd say. The same crook was later blasted to death with a shotgun in a shop doorway in Bridgeton.

There were plenty of robberies at that time and sometimes the raiders were masked. At one point, a bookies in the Cowcaddens area was hit. One of the crooks was wearing a mask designed to look like US President Ronald Reagan. We heard a message on the AS (All Stations) radio system – 'Be on the lookout for Ronald Reagan' in his getaway car. We laughed at the absurdity of it but it paid off.

A detective sergeant who was driving through the city was amazed to see Ronald Reagan approaching at speed in a vehicle coming the other way. The daft robber had forgotten to take his mask off when he'd jumped into the getaway car! The drama of the occasion must have been too much for him and his accomplices hadn't noticed how presidential he was looking.

The gang was nicked and unmasked. Interestingly, on that occasion, the thief with the mask was of Chinese extraction. It was common to find that masked robbers came from ethnic minorities because they obviously stood out among the general population. We knew most of the bad boys in the various ethnic groups, which also made it easier to find out who was behind the crimes if a member of those communities was suspected.

A call came in to report there was a full-term, newborn baby dead in a house. Was it a stillbirth or a murder? When I got there uniformed officers were on the scene and the distraught mother was still in the flat. She tearfully told me that she hadn't been due to give birth for a while but had felt there was something wrong with the unborn tot as the pregnancy didn't feel normal for some reason. She'd had children before. That day she had suffered stomach pains and felt an urgent sensation before giving birth unexpectedly.

A doctor was on his way to support the traumatised mother. My sad task was to work out if she was telling the truth or if foul play was involved in the baby's death. Scenes of crime officers photographed and preserved the place. The mother was taken to hospital to be checked out and I tried to organise suitable transport to have the tot taken for a post-mortem.

But undertakers couldn't provide anyone quickly to take the little body to the Queen Mother's maternity hospital, which had the unique role of doing post-mortems on babies. I had arranged the procedure and the busy staff were ready to proceed. I couldn't wait for three hours or more at the house until transport arrived. So I made a tough decision. I would take the baby to the hospital myself. After ensuring the premises were secure, I put the tot's body in a poly bag and placed it carefully in the boot of the CID car.

At the hospital I watched my first PM of a baby. One crucial piece of evidence emerged. The doctor held the tot's hand in front of a powerful lamp and asked me to observe the fingers. He explained that blood hadn't reached the fingertips, meaning the heart hadn't been pumping it to the body's extremities. He was convinced it was a stillbirth. It was a relief to hear the death wasn't murder and the mum was in the clear. After the post-mortem the hospital arranged for the baby to be placed in a chapel in the building.

I felt the events had been handled well. The tragic mum had been spared from seeing her baby again and I could confirm to her that we knew it was a stillbirth.

It was routine for an officer involved in such cases to go to the funeral. On this occasion I put myself forward as the repre-sentative of the force. But what a shock I got when I attended the service! It was the biggest funeral I'd ever been to, with a huge number of family, friends and well-wishers. I was amazed that all those people were there for a little baby they'd never known.

As I saw the tiny coffin carried in the church, I began to wonder about my handling of the case. What would the mour-ners have thought if they'd known I had carried the tot's body in a much less reverential way – in a plastic bag? And that I had put it in the boot of a car and driven through the streets?

Had I done the wrong thing? Maybe all the deaths I'd seen had desensitised me to the tragedy? Perhaps I should have waited for the funeral directors to arrive. But I knew from past experience they sometimes didn't handle bodies any more sensitively in these situations. I felt justified because I had found the answers about the death quickly and had ended what could have become a major inquiry. Perhaps I would have got into trouble if senior management had found out the process. The baby death investigation was an emotional incident that gave me pause for thought.

Then there was the time that the theft of a video recorder by a Glasgow ned led to the arrest of a pair of international crooks who'd carried out a massive cash heist. In December 1984, I went to a house in the Southside of Glasgow. I'd been there before and knew the family had some problems but were basically decent folk. I'd been called out by the daughter, who was in her mid-twenties, and had just moved into her first flat. She complained that her younger brother had sneaked in while she was out and pinched her VCR before doing a runner. It was a fairly minor crime but I got his details circulated.

Towards the end of January, I was surprised to get a call from the cops in Cornwall. They'd picked up the boy in Newquay where he'd been having a blast with some of his pals before their fun had ended when they'd had a car crash. The cops had found £300 in £20 notes in his pocket. They couldn't tie it in to any thefts in their area so wondered if he'd nicked the money in Glasgow.

I went back to the sister to see if she could shed any light on the money. She took a deep breath and admitted, 'There's something I haven't told you.' Then she outlined an unlikely tale. She explained that she'd been at the bus station in the city with a pal at New Year. As they'd sat in the cafe, they'd got chatting to two men who had just arrived in town and were carting suitcases. The two guys said they were looking for a place to stay so the girls had coupled up with the men and taken them to their homes.

The blokes had eventually confessed they were international thieves who'd pinched nearly a million dollars in different currency from Frankfurt Airport in Germany. It turned out the cases were stuffed with cash. The fugitives had spent lavishly on the women, paying for new electrical goods and doing up their homes. There certainly was plenty of money in those suitcases.

181

The men had claimed they'd stolen the fortune in a cunning raid. Their story was they'd hit airline premises where international currency was stored. They'd both claimed to have been employed as security experts at the depot, allowing them to disable alarms and pull off the heist. Then they'd done a runner to lie low and check the currency they'd looted. They'd kept hold of the dollars, pounds and marks but had to dump the currency they couldn't easily exchange. So they'd stuck it in litter bins in Germany!

After flying from Germany to London, they'd checked the departures board and decided to visit Scotland and have a low-key stay in Glasgow. When they'd arrived in the city on the bus from the airport they'd met the local girls.

The sister reckoned her wee brother had come back to her flat after his theft of the VCR and seen some of the money poking out of her man's suitcase. He had just helped himself to a handful before running off. It wouldn't have been missed by the robber because he had so much cash.

By this time the two men had left their girlfriends. We tracked down the raiders. One was in Glasgow's Central Hotel and we grabbed him and I recovered money in a safety deposit box in a local bank. The other guy was found in a hotel in Edinburgh by the cops there. They discovered plenty of cash with him. We brought them in for questioning and I got hold of contacts in Germany to speak to about the case. But I had to go on holiday and couldn't follow it through. It was passed to another officer and the men were eventually taken to London where they were extradited.

I thought I was getting a trip to Germany to appear as a witness but I never heard any more. Some time later someone told me they thought the two bandits had pled guilty. The only record there is of a cash robbery at Frankfurt Airport in December 1984 isn't quite as sophisticated as the men described.

A thief made off with two bags containing the equivalent of nearly a million dollars as the money was being unloaded from a

Yugoslav plane. Police said the man drove up in a white bus, marked 'Finnair', as six ground crew members were off-loading the cash. The crook sprang out of the vehicle and grabbed the two money bags and, before racing away, fired a tear gas charge in the face of a worker who was trying to stop him. Cops said the robbery was so well organised they suspected more than one person could be involved. The thief must have had prior knowledge that the cash was on the plane.

The case shows how a major crime can be solved through attention to detail when dealing with a minor offence.

17

A BRUTAL ROBBER
AND MURDER WITH A MAGNUM

I was keeping my eyes and ears open around the Hampden Park area of Glasgow one day, about August 1985. My sights focused on a character wandering around suspiciously. He was a time-served housebreaker who was out of his home patch. He was up to no good, I reckoned, and intercepted him before he could case any more potential targets.

His face fell when he clocked me. He knew I'd soon be sticking my nose into what he'd been up to around the district, sniffing out crimes that could have his name on them. But he had an ace up his sleeve. He was also one of my informants and he decided to give me some juicy information to placate me and no doubt try to distract me from his own dodgy activities.

He began to lay out a dramatic tale about an armed robbery not far from there a few days before. Four men, three masked, burst into the Martex cash & carry in Polmadie Road. Armed with knives, they handcuffed the manager, who was on his own, and tied him up with rope. To get him to play ball they held knives to his throat, punched and kicked him and threatened to chop his fingers off. They grabbed a load of cigarettes and cigars and scooped up £40 from the till.

Their efforts to get hold of a key to the safe failed as the manager bravely refused to succumb to their threats and hand it over it to them. There was £30,000 locked in there but they couldn't get at it. They left behind a number of items that could possibly help us, including some pieces of rope.

My tout mentioned the names of four people allegedly caught up in the blag. All of them had a colourful criminal history. One was a character called James Boyce. I got hold of warrants to search all four homes and we discovered cigarettes and cigars and pieces of rope in Boyce's place. That allowed us to detain him and charge him with armed robbery. Boyce had been the only one who was unmasked and the victim could easily identify the brute who'd attacked him.

In his mid-forties, he was a bit of a beast, but not aggressive towards me and not as intimidating as some could be. I recall he wasn't particularly cooperative but he was an old-school criminal, who knew that if the investigation was done properly, he had to take his medicine. A case of don't do the crime if you can't do the time.

He was charged but we couldn't get enough evidence against the other three to put them in the dock alongside him. The case went to trial at the High Court in Airdrie. The manager gave detailed and emotional testimony about his horrific ordeal. But at one point the prosecutor appeared to be losing hope that we could get a conviction. He was thinking about abandoning the case due to lack of evidence. I told him I'd been watching the jury closely and they seemed like an upright, intelligent bunch who were showing a close interest in the proceedings. I asked him if he'd carry on and, thankfully, he decided to give it a whirl.

Boyce was found guilty of assault and robbery by a majority and given five years. Two years into his stretch he escaped from jail but was recaptured and given 18 months for the break-out. However, his notoriety was far from over. His name came to my attention again in 1993. A former colleague from the Scottish Crime Squad called and told me he was investigating Boyce over a brutal and ruthless crime which left a German tourist dead and his wife and daughter badly injured.

Having passed on my best advice to the other cop, I learned more about the attack. The murder of Thomas Boedeker and Boyce's savage attack on the victim's family stunned the quiet community of Cairnryan, near Stranraer.

Architect Mr Boedeker, who was 53, was on holiday with his wife Renate, 48, and their children Julia, 20, and 15-year-old son Just. They'd been getting ready to leave their campsite and head for home after their four-week holiday, when they encountered the violent Boyce.

He approached Mr Boedeker, who was from Stuttgart, shouting, 'Money, money!' Boyce terrified the family, waving about a .45-calibre wartime revolver and a large kitchen knife. Before the German tourist could say anything, Boyce fired two shots at him. As Mr Boedeker slumped to the ground, blood pouring from wounds to his arm and stomach, his distraught daughter fished her father's wallet from his trouser pocket and passed it to Boyce as her hand shook with fear.

Her actions didn't appease crazed Boyce and he blasted her in the leg and thigh. Mrs Boedeker was then shot in the upper body and, as he tried to flee the scene, Just felt a bullet tear into his right arm.

Apparently desperate to ensure there were no surviving witnesses to his mayhem, Boyce began to lash out with his knife. He targeted the two women, stabbing Julia three times in the back, piercing a lung. Her mother was repeatedly stabbed, the blows so violent that her ribs were broken. After Boyce made off, Just managed to raise the alarm.

Boyce, who'd been working as a bus cleaner since leaving jail, admitted at the High Court in Glasgow that he'd murdered Mr Boedeker and attempted to murder of his wife and two children. He also pleaded guilty to robbing them amid the bloodbath at the Cairnryan campsite. The judge gave him to two life sentences – a minimum of 20 years.

There was TV coverage of him leaving the court on his way to jail. I recall watching it with my wife. As the savage-looking

Boyce snarled at the camera, my better half commented, 'I wouldn't like to meet him up a dark alley!' I broke the news to her that I'd personally encountered the frightening individual in my previous adventures. As I set off to do a late shift that night, it occurred to me that my wife probably had no idea of some of the things that went on in my work.

Eight years later, Boyce, who was originally from Rutherglen, near Glasgow, put in a bizarre request for a jail move to Northern Ireland. He wanted out of the Scottish prison system and into the notorious Maze Prison in Belfast, home to terrorist prisoners. It was reported that he had claimed to have relatives in the country and to have been involved in a Provo gun-running team. It was claimed he'd hoped to be taken under the wing of members of the Ulster Defence Association.

That bid failed and he spent time in tough Shotts Prison in Lanarkshire, a maximum security unit that is home to some of the hardest criminals in the country. But there was controversy when his sentence was cut on appeal to 17 years and he was eventually moved to Castle Huntly open prison to prepare for freedom.

Outrage erupted in 2008 when a newspaper photographed Boyce buying ice cream in Shotts village while on unsupervised release with another jailbird. The pair had been tidying the prison car park before their lunchtime jaunt. Asked how he felt about his crimes, Boyce apparently said his past misdemeanours made him feel emotional and that saying sorry was never enough.

It's a difficult question for society. Should a man who was given two life terms ever get out? He killed one person and tried to murder three others. Does a man with such a horrendous set of convictions deserve any sympathy and the right to walk about free?

Hair of the dog can sometimes cure a headache caused by a hangover. But there was one occasion when I reckoned hair off a dog could help me cure my headache over an unsolved case.

In July 1986 a family were relaxing at home in Gorbals when there was a knock at the door. The female householder opened it and was terrified to be confronted by two masked men, who forced their way into the living room. As one of them held a blade to her throat, they threatened to kill her if she didn't tell them where her money was kept. As her shocked son looked on, she boldly refused. So the violent intruders made their point clearer, slashing her on both hands. Her horrified son then handed over a purse with £70 in it and the raiders scarpered.

I was soon on the case, getting the family's version of events before searching the surrounding area to see if the purse had been dumped. We hit pay-dirt in a nearby close. In a blue poly bag we discovered the purse – but more than that. It looked like we'd found gear worn by the robbers. There was a navy blue boiler-suit, a pair of green denim trousers, three training shoes, four odd socks and, crucially, an open razor. Not far away we found the other trainer and two black nylon tights – presumably the masks they'd worn.

Some of the clothing was reckoned to be similar to what a well-known housebreaker had been wearing when last arrested a couple of weeks before. It was also thought a similar boiler-suit had been spotted in his home at the time.

The victims knew this man and he fitted the physical description of one of the masked robbers. To add to our suspicions, a member of the family had recently innocently told him that the mother kept cash in the house.

We got the forensic boys to take a look at the gear we'd turned up. There were a few possible clues. There were paint spots on the boiler-suit. The socks had carpet fibres on them and one of the masks had hair sticking to it. There was also hair on the socks – longer than normal and grey-brown. That got me thinking. I'd been in this guy's home before and I knew he had a big Alsatian dog, which had hair that same colour.

I got a warrant to search the man's home. I was after paint samples to match the boiler-suit spots, some carpet pile and any socks matching the odd ones we'd discovered. I also needed a sample of his head hair. But by far the most unusual item on the list was permission to take a sample of the dug's hair.

A young cop accompanied me to the criminal's home to carry out the unlikely assignment of clipping some hair from the Alsatian. Fortunately, the dog didn't object to its trim although its owner looked a bit surprised that Fido had been caught up in the robbery allegations.

The results came back. The hair we had suspected was from the dog was indeed non-human. Could they tell us any more? Was it from a dog? Sorry, they said, we don't know. A doggy DNA database would have come in handy but there wasn't even one for humans back then. The best you could get was a blood group. The experts told us the human hair was similar and the carpet fibres could have been from the same rug.

None of it was enough for me in my attempt to lock up our man on that occasion. My inventive attempt to use hairy socks to sock it to a suspect hadn't worked. It was an idea too advanced for the science of the time.

A gunshot rang out and two men slumped to the floor of the bar. The .357 bullet from the monster gun – a 'Dirty Harry' Magnum – had ripped through one customer's body and then blasted into a second drinker.

The first victim, 49-year-old James Nelson, died from the bullet in his chest. Ambulance crew had battled to save him at the scene to no avail. Incredibly, the unfortunate drinker who had become collateral damage, John Sweeney, was still alive. He had a miraculous escape after being hit in the back as he sat close by. A rib deflected the bullet past his kidneys, liver and lungs. The spent bullet was found lying on the pub floor.

The location of the crime, in November 1986, was the Victoria Bar in Crosshill, Glasgow. I raced to the pub to examine the Wild West scene. The bar and surrounding streets were cordoned off. I'd seen many gunshot wounds but this was different. One bullet claiming two victims in a split second was a new one on me.

It soon became apparent who the shooter was. An anonymous call came in to the control room, giving a nickname – 'Stab Eddie'. He was a dangerous character we knew well. His real name was Edward Burke. He'd got his gruesome moniker because he'd been convicted in 1967, aged just 19, of knifing another teenager to death in Glasgow's Buchanan Street. Unfortunately for society, Stab Eddie been released on licence after less than ten years.

Burke had come to our attention some time before the shooting when he'd turned up in Gorbals. He was from Cumbernauld and the locals didn't like the incomer. He'd got a reputation as a troublemaker and we'd heard about him from folk who wanted a lid put on his activities. It was unusual at the time, as the local bad boys were normally able to keep their area under control.

Burke, according to informants, often carried a knife and was running about with it, upsetting the normal balance of criminal life in the Gorbals area. When the blade wasn't on him, we were told, he stashed it in the ladies' toilet of a certain pub, concealing it in the cistern of one of the loos. We'd checked out the info but couldn't find the weapon when we searched the toilet. Burke didn't take kindly to our interest in him and objected to being stopped and checked out. He'd put in a complaint, through his lawyer, accusing Gorbals CID of harassing him.

Complaints were a problem for officers because they could curtail promotion prospects while they dragged on. And the investigations could go on for a long time. Senior uniformed officers from the complaints department would call the cop in for an interview. Standard procedure for the officer under fire was to give the brass no comment and refuse to hand over notebooks, explaining they formed part of criminal proceedings. The officer under investigation would provide his or her formal statement and request that the matter be dealt with as soon as possible as it cast a shadow over career prospects.

Being on the mean streets was tough and it was part of the job description that complaints would be lodged against cops. If you didn't want people moaning about you, it was best to stay away from the coal face. No matter how straight and hard-working they were, officers on the front line would invariably attract a complaint from a discontented person, probably criminal.

Now Stab Eddie's gripes didn't look so justified. It appeared we had been right to keep such close tabs on him as he was in the frame for a brutal and unusual gun crime.

We were on a roll. Having identified the suspect from his well-known nickname, we got a call from another anonymous informant. The info was that the murder weapon had been hidden – in a familiar way. It was said to be in the cistern of a toilet in the ladies at a nearby pub, the Queen's Park Café Bar in Victoria Road. That method of concealment sounded like it had Stab's fingerprints all over it.

I headed to the unfamiliar surroundings of the women's toilets in the bar and quickly found the gun. It was a monstrous weapon and I'd never seen anything like it. How Burke had got it into the ladies, we didn't know. Maybe a female friend had taken it in for him or perhaps he'd just walked into there, bold as brass.

Despite our previous interest in him, we had never found out where Stab Eddie was living. But I got another break that night. Around midnight I bumped into a local who knew Burke's reputation. This person was able to give me an address – the high flats in Waddell Court in Gorbals. We got a posse together and prepared to grab our man.

There was a four-legged addition to our team. A new policy meant the dog branch had to be brought in when we were tackling potentially armed and dangerous criminals. We weren't entirely happy with the presence of the sharp-toothed dug. How would Bonzo know the difference between a criminal and a criminal investigator during the heat of an arrest? We didn't want it sinking its fangs into us so we convinced the dog handler to stay by the front door. It was the likeliest escape route given we were several floors up and an exit through the window wasn't on for our man.

It was 4.15am when we burst into the two-storey flat. We found Stab Eddie asleep downstairs. Beside him was a copy of the early edition of that day's *Daily Record*, detailing his crime on the front page. 'SHOT IN COLD BLOOD' screamed the headline. 'Man dies in pub horror,' it said alongside. Had Burke been enjoying reading about his murderous handiwork or absorbing just how serious his situation had become?

There was no time for a polite discussion in those situations. We didn't know if the gun we had found was his. What if he had a shooter in his hand? And what if Stab lived up to his name by wielding a knife? Before he had properly woken up he was pounced on to subdue him. The handcuffs were snapped on him and he came quietly as the female householder, who'd been sleeping upstairs, watched in horror.

With Burke in custody, the details of the mayhem in the bar that night unfolded from the lips of witnesses. A shocked customer said he'd gone to the bar to sell tickets for a football lottery when he'd heard an argument among a group of men at a table. The witness reckoned one of them had shouted, 'Put that gun away or I'll shove it up your arse!' The publican had calmed them down but then there had been a shot and he'd seen Burke in a crouching position, holding a long-barrelled revolver.

The witness said Stab Eddie had strolled out of the pub as others watched in stunned silence. The customer was horrified when he realised the man lying dead on the floor was Mr Nelson, who'd bought a lottery ticket – just before his luck ran out.

One of the men who'd been sitting at the same table as Burke said he had seen him bring out the gun and warned him to put it away. He'd turned round to speak to Mr Sweeney at a table behind when he'd heard a bang and witnessed the victim stop talking and fall from his seat.

A pal of Stab had run into him in the Queen's Park Café Bar not long after and Burke had asked him for a lift to Gorbals. The friend said Burke had confessed he'd shot someone and the driver recalled putting his foot down after they passed the cop cars outside the crime scene. A female friend of Burke admitted he'd confessed to the shooting as he walked with her to a local bar following his arrival at her home at 8pm. He'd taken her back to the Queen's Park Bar later but she'd left when he'd visited the toilet. Burke had come back to her house later and rested on the settee in the living room until our troops arrived in our early morning operation.

Burke denied murdering Mr Nelson and attempting to murder Mr Sweeney. At the 38-year-old's trial, a pathologist outlined the terrifying force of the Magnum bullet. It had torn through the first man's heart and lungs before exiting through his back, hitting the man sitting behind him.

Stab Eddie was given life for the bizarre twin attack. He was also found guilty of three contraventions of the Firearms Act. Of course, life doesn't mean life. Burke got out in 2002, freed under European Human Rights legislation, which gives lifers the right to a set tariff. A year later, Burke was back in trouble. No knives or guns this time. Now it was drugs.

He'd teamed up with another pair of jailbirds. One was a drug smuggler, the other had killed a nightwatchman during a payroll theft on a Glasgow rail depot in 1973. The trio were caught in a raid by the Scottish Drug Enforcement Agency, despite their futile attempts to cover up their crime with a dopey attempt to chuck £50,000 of cocaine out of the sixth-floor window of a Coatbridge flat. Cops standing below picked up the bin bag full of evidence. The drug was over 80 per cent pure and the three men were said to be at the top of the distribution chain. Stab Eddie was soon back behind bars, this time for seven years.

An individual reported a housebreaking – but I wasn't overly sympathetic. In fact, I didn't believe a word he said. I knew the man and had sized him up as an arrogant and cheeky type whose honesty was in question. I arrived at his home from the Gorbals office and listened patiently as he told me someone had kicked in his front door and his TV, video and other large electrical items had been pinched. Aye, right!

As routine dictated, scenes of crime officers came and had a good look about. But there were no unidentified fingerprints and the busted door was the only evidence. I checked with the neighbours and they said they'd heard a bang – probably when the door was put in. But they hadn't seen anyone raiding the place or removing property.

My doubts grew and I decided to go back the following morning to see if the man had anything fresh to tell me – and, ideally, to catch him on the hop. When I got there with my colleague, we found the door was still broken. I knocked loudly and it creaked open. But there was no response from the householder.

Given that I had met the man and was investigating a crime, I felt it appropriate to go inside to ensure he wasn't there. I noted something I hadn't seen the day before. The couch had been moved forward and was askew. I took a look – and found a treasure trove. There, behind the sofa, was all the stolen property he'd listed to me and told the insurance company was missing. It didn't surprise me and we beat a retreat down the stairs and waited outside in the car until the crook came home.

When we arrived on his doorstep again he said he couldn't invite us in as he didn't have time to speak. That was just what I wanted to hear. There was a small possibility the stuff behind the couch was new equipment he'd bought to replace the stolen gear, although it would have been a strange place to keep it. But his evasive behaviour convinced me that was not the case. We strode past him and had a look around, pretending to notice the displaced couch for the first time. When his hidden booty was revealed the crook became abusive and obstructive.

He picked up the phone and called his solicitor. He ranted and raved to the lawyer that we had kicked in his door – and planted the property to frame him! He also claimed we'd assaulted and verbally abused him. I took the phone and spoke to the brief who, unbeknown to the criminal, I knew quite well. As the householder watched me, with steam coming out of his ears, I told the solicitor, 'Don't come down to the station until this evening. I will be quite a while with your client as he will be arrested and will be appearing in court in the morning.'

That sent the man loopy but the lawyer understood the situation. Our suspect was charged with attempting to pervert the course of justice and pled not guilty before putting in a complaint about us, alleging we'd fitted him up. Of course, I then faced another investigation by the 'rubber heels' and had the shadow of the false accusation hanging over me.

But when his case came to court he changed his plea to guilty. I was delighted and quickly called the Complaints and Discipline guys to tell them and insist the complaint was scrubbed from their list. The whole episode was a tough lesson in how going to help someone can backfire on a police officer.

18

THE KNIFEMAN AND THE PRIEST, THE WAILING WALL AND A SKELETON IN PYJAMAS

I was glad I had a big colleague with me when we went to arrest two suspects over a violent assault. The pair didn't come quietly and we had to drag them out of their home. Perhaps it wasn't surprising as they knew they could be facing a long sentence for their brutal attack on an Asian man. They'd battered their victim so savagely that he'd lost an eye. He was a bus driver and the injury meant he'd had to leave his job.

The beating of the driver was so severe that they were charged with attempted murder. At court, the defence tried to lessen their potential punishment by saying they would plead guilty to a reduced charge of serious assault. That way they'd probably be looking at doing four or five years. But the neds hadn't taken into account that a new judge was on the bench and looking to make an impact in his first case. He'd obviously decided he wanted to establish a tough reputation among the lords of the High Court. I was as stunned as the open-mouthed defendants when he pronounced their sentences – twelve years each! There were gasps all round. They'd probably have got less on a murder charge.

After the heavy sanction, I spoke to the bus driver and passed on my sympathies for the injuries and trauma he'd suffered. But I told him, 'At least there must be some satisfaction in seeing your attackers get put away for so long.' Then came the second sensational utterance of the day. 'The sentences are far too long. They shouldn't have got that,' he told me. I was left reeling and wondering to myself what I had to do to ensure people were happy with the way justice was delivered.

I was wandering through the police station in Gorbals late one night when I saw an unusual sight. A man was standing at the front door, holding a huge Bowie-style knife to his own throat. The blade on the weapon was enormous and he was rooted to the spot, eyes glazed and hand trembling.

It was 2am and the officer at the front desk, the only other person on duty, was calmly watching the unfolding madness. The lunatic visitor didn't seem to notice me in his trance-like state so I headed upstairs to the CID office to tackle the situation out of sight. I phoned the officer downstairs, who said he was alright. 'What does the guy want?' I asked. 'No idea. He's no' saying anything,' came the reply.

I went down to the scene and took charge of the bizarre situation. We called an ambulance to ensure there was medical help if the man cut his throat or launched an attack on me and my colleague. The local beat officers were ordered to return to the station by the back door to provide assistance and to see if they could identify the man. One was stationed outside the front of the office to make sure no members of the public stumbled into the dangerous stand-off.

One of the bobbies recognised the knifeman. He had been seen in the company of a local Italian man and it was thought he had an Italian name. By now it was 3am and I wasn't sure how to bring the drama to an end. I tried to reason with him and keep him calm. I asked him to confirm his identity but he said nothing and just stared into space. I came to the conclusion he was either deaf, ignoring me or simply didn't speak English. Perhaps he only knew Italian.

None of us were familiar with the Romance languages so I hit upon a plan to try to get through to him. 'Head up to the chapel and see if you can find a priest who speaks Italian,' I instructed one of the PCs. After a nervous wait as the man continued his display, the cop returned with a flustered-looking padre who could talk Italian.

Father rubbed the sleep out of his eyes and looked at the crazed intruder through a two-way mirror. He said he wasn't one of his flock and he'd never seen him before. I implored to him to have a go at speaking to the man to try to find out what his problem was and where his family were. The priest bravely stepped out in front of the blade-wielding visitor and began preaching his message of peace.

He spoke in suitably animated 'mamma mia' Italian, waving his arms as he pleaded with the man to explain his predicament. I watched the intruder's face closely and saw it switch from fear and anger to a look of quizzical confusion. The priest's sermon seemed to have had some effect on the man and suddenly he threw his knife to the floor and spoke for the first time – in a strong Glasgow accent. 'Why the f*ck is he speaking to me in Italian? I don't speak Italian. And I'm not even a f*cking Catholic!' he bellowed.

We overpowered him and picked up the knife as he looked at us in confusion. 'What did I do?' he demanded, seemingly having no memory of events. 'I remember I fell out with the wife and decided to kill myself.' He'd stumbled into the police office the worse for drink and held the knife to his throat in his stupor.

We calmed him down, sent the ambulance away and got his family to collect him. My memory is that he was charged with possession of a knife but wasn't accused of a breach of the peace because the offence couldn't take place in a police station where only cops are present. After all, officers are supposed to be used to the crazy behaviour of the general public. I certainly was, but that incident stood out among the unusual ones. We later managed to have a good laugh about the pantomime of the priest chattering in Italian to the baffled knifeman.

There was a stushie after a member of the public went into a police office and spotted a girlie calendar on display. The woman was outraged by the topless pictures and complained. An order came down from Chief Constable Andrew Sloan: all nudey calendars had to be removed from the walls of police stations.

I happened to be on late shift in Gorbals that night and was the senior detective covering the division. The detective superintendent gave me the unusual task of ensuring the cheeky calendars were taken down in all the CID offices. I had a good look around my own workplace and found no sign of any topless glamour girls.

Next, I headed to Craigie Street and went hunting for half-naked dolly birds. The premises were given the all-clear and I moved on to the Pollokshaws station. The cops there had disposed of their titillating calendars as well. I left Rutherglen until last as I knew I'd be offered a coffee there. Once again, the calendars had been removed. As I sat enjoying my coffee, I pondered how responsible and helpful the boys had been in taking down their naughty pictures from the workplace. Just then, I glanced upwards and I nearly dropped my drink in surprise.

The ceiling of the CID office was plastered with pictures of topless women! Every saucy photo from the whole place had been gathered up and stuck there. The cops had interpreted the order from the chief literally. The calendars had indeed been removed from the walls. The ceiling didn't count, in their view. I wrote a note outlining my discovery and left it to someone else to pull down the pics. It was a classic example of police humour.

When computerisation came in, it changed our relationship with the prosecutors. We began emailing our reports to the fiscals, which cut out the personal contact we'd enjoyed until then. The old way was to go the fiscals' office and outline the case directly to them. That way they got to know and trust us. More importantly, we got to know them – which ones were weak and who was a smart operator. Then we could avoid the less impressive ones.

If we were dealing with people already in custody we'd speak to members of the 'summary team', perhaps asking for more time to hold the suspect to gather evidence. They sat in a reception area which we called the Wailing Wall because we went there to make our custody case pleas to them. Minor offences went to police court or district court, bigger ones went to the sheriff court.

If, however, we were looking for a warrant to arrest someone or discussing an ongoing case with the fiscal, we'd be called into their offices. One of my favourite characters always welcomed you in and it was particularly interesting if you turned up during his break time. He was a rail fanatic and had a large model train set in his office. The tunnels were made from law books. It was amusing to watch his choo-choos going round as we discussed serious criminal matters, and he was a joy to know.

Seeing them face-to-face meant you could negotiate with them a bit. One person got his wheels and tyres stolen from his car. I recovered them from a suspect, who denied the theft, and the fiscal reckoned there was no way to prove they were the same tyres. We both agreed we weren't experts on cars but I told him the complainer was. He'd identified his stolen wheels from marks on them as if he was studying fingerprints. The prosecutor agreed to give it a go and the ned pled guilty to nicking them.

Another time, a head teacher at a secondary school was facing an assault charge for striking a pupil. There was no doubt the cheeky schoolboy had been hit but it was a very minor offence and he'd not been marked or injured. The teacher was in hysterics as he was about to retire and feared a terrible blot on his career. A senior officer asked me if I could do anything. I went to one of the fiscals I knew and outlined my point of view. The teacher was, by the accounts of all who knew him, an upstanding member of the community. The assault had happened but was minor. The man had only a few more days in the job so wouldn't be in that situation again. I apologised for even asking and said it was a difficult situation, but I hoped the fiscal would take into account the circumstances I'd outlined. The case was marked 'no proeedings', much to the delight of the teacher and my colleague.

One funny moment came after the Old College Bar, which is apparently the oldest pub in Glasgow, was held up by masked raiders. I dictated my report to the fiscal into a tape recorder and it was passed to a typist to transcribe and email it. In my summary of the offence, I said the barmaid had been by the till when the men had burst in. She had noticed one of them had a distinctive, gravelly voice – useful for the later ID parade. I dictated, 'One of the youths said, in a gruff voice, "Give us the money".' Next morning I got a puzzled call from the fiscal. He didn't understand the strange order the barmaid had been given by the robbers. He explained the report said she'd been told, 'In a gruff voice give us the money.' The typist must have been having a bad day as her punctuation was a bit out.

There was an uncomfortable occasion when we had to tell the fiscals about criminal complaints against an unlikely suspect – one of their own colleagues. We were working on a case involving female witnesses. One of the DCs came to me and said he'd received a complaint from one of the witnesses who had been interviewed by Glasgow's top fiscal, John Skeen. Imagine our shock when she reported to us that the respected prosecutor had allegedly touched her inappropriately while they'd been alone together. The investigation was passed to Strathclyde Police officers as it didn't fall under the remit of the Scottish Crime Squad. The Strathclyde cops then spoke to two other women who claimed the fiscal had made inappropriate comments to them.

The police file on the highly sensitive investigation was passed to the Crown Office for the consideration of the Crown Agent – the legal advisor to the Lord Advocate, Scotland's top prosecutor. Not long after, 61-year-old Mr Skeen announced his early retirement on medical grounds. He'd previously had a heart attack but had returned to work after the scare. Colleagues paid tribute to him as he took his leave but his reputation was soon under threat of being tarnished when the press got hold of the story about the allegations against him.

When the furore broke in September 1980, furious Mr Skeen tried to withdraw his resignation. But the Lord Advocate refused his request. Then came an unprecedented public statement from the Crown Office, clarifying the course of events. It said the three women had complained to police, one of them saying Mr Skeen had 'touched her body on top of her clothing'. The remarkable statement went on, 'All three complained of the words used by Mr Skeen. In the case of one woman, the words alleged to have been used would not have amounted to a crime, if proved. But in the case of the other two, they might, if proved, have amounted to a breach of the peace.'

The announcement said Mr Skeen had protested his innocence and the women had stuck to their stories. It continued, 'The two who alleged criminal conduct made it clear, however, that for personal reasons they did not want the publicity which would ensue if they were called as witnesses against Mr Skeen in a criminal trial. After careful consideration of the allegations, and being advised that no other complaints had been received, the Lord Advocate accepted Mr Skeen's resignation and decided not to institute any proceedings in respect of these complaints against Mr Skeen.'

The Crown Office insisted the women were happy with the outcome and rejected newspaper claims that others had come forward to complain about the fiscal's alleged behaviour. Amid a barrage of questions from reporters, Crown Agent William

Chalmers was asked if some people would see the statement as a 'whitewash'. He replied, 'If they do, it's up to them.'

One MP said it must be established whether prosecutors had been trying to protect one of their own. Dennis Canavan said, 'The public are entitled to the assurance that there is not one law for procurators fiscal and another law for the rest of us.' Solicitor William Dunn, who was working for the defence in the original case the women were involved in, was astonished. He said, 'If witnesses had to call off giving evidence for so-called personal reasons, there would never be any cases brought to court.'

It's worth pointing out that Mr Skeen was never prosecuted or found guilty of anything, despite the allegations being made public. The Law Society of Scotland highlighted that point, saying, 'What must give cause for concern is the fact that a prominent and highly-respected public figure finds himself publicly the subject of serious allegations – which he denies absolutely – and he has no opportunity to vindicate himself in open court.'

Next, the row moved to the highest echelons of politics. There was a debate about the 'Glasgow Fiscal Affair' in the House of Lords. Their lordships, however, seemed more concerned about how the information had been leaked to the press and why the statement had been made, rather than the handling of the allegations. The Lord Advocate told them it was impossible to say if the police had leaked the story. I am convinced there was no leak from my colleagues in the Scottish Crime Squad. He explained he had named Mr Skeen to assure members of the public dealing with the fiscal service that they weren't going to encounter the prosecutor at the centre of the claims. Asked if anything was known about the 'character' of the women that might put their claims in doubt, the Lord Advocate declined to go into detail about them.

One of the most horrific sights I saw was the gruesome vision of a man sitting up in bed in his pyjamas – more than two years after he'd died. I was confronted with the bizarre scene while a DS in Gorbals. The uniform boys had discovered a dead body and weren't sure if foul play was part of the picture.

I headed to the flat with my DI and was met with a tragic situation. As soon as we got into the place we knew we weren't dealing with a fresh corpse. The entire house was covered in dead bluebottles. The window sills were inches thick with them.

In the bedroom, we saw what had attracted them over the months before. The skeletal figure of man was on the bed, his pyjama top done up to his neck. He seemed to be staring at me, a patch of hair still on his head. But that was all that was left. The nightwear formed a chilling shell around his bones. All flesh and muscle had long since disappeared. Perhaps a good thing for us, as the choking stench of rotting flesh was long gone from the room.

We had a good look at the situation to work out if he'd been murdered. There was no sign of a bullet or damage from one on his skeleton. No ligature around his neck bone. Given the way he was seated, it appeared he'd died naturally and peacefully although, I recall, he was probably only in his fifties. The medical experts reckoned he could have been there for a couple of years or more.

It was sad to think he'd remained there so long, slowly decomposing. Surprising, too, that family, neighbours, visitors to the house and the authorities hadn't noticed his absence or the tell-tale smell of a dead body after he passed away. It showed how death in the city could be lonely as well as tragic.

There were too many armed robberies and guns on the street for our liking in the late 1980s. To calm public concern, one of our senior officers undertook a press conference to announce that a special team of armed officers would be on alert 24 hours a day.

He was hit by a barrage of questions.

'How many will be on duty?' shouted a hack.

'Four at any one time, sometimes more,' the cop replied.

'What guns will they have?' demanded another journalist.

'Smith & Wesson .38 revolvers,' he confirmed.

'What will the new initiative be called?' another reporter asked.

Watching the TV, we all took an interest because, as far as we knew, it hadn't been given a name. But the officer remained cool and, thinking on his feet, managed to come up with something impressive-sounding on the spot. 'It will be known as the Fast Action Response Team.'

It took a moment for us all to work out the unwelcome acronym we'd just been given. We had a laugh about it but we got a bit fed up of being mocked by other cops who called us the Fart Squad. But we managed to have a major impact on getting rid of the armed robbers. You could say the Fart Squad put the wind up them!

19

CRIMINAL INTELLIGENCE AND CRIMESTOPPERS, A CANNABIS CROP AND THE ESTONIAN VISITORS

In 1989, I was promoted to Detective Inspector and took up my new and exciting role as head of Strathclyde's Criminal Intelligence Department. Having intelligence files on potential and known crooks was a vital addition to the criminal records we held. I took a great interest in the discipline of criminal intelligence and its history.

It began in the police service at the beginning of the 1950s with the formation of C9 Branch at New Scotland Yard in London, which helped officers from the Home Counties with the investigation of burglaries and robberies thought to have been committed by criminals based in the capital.

By the late 1950s travelling criminals had become a serious problem and it was predicted that the opening of the M1 motorway in 1959 would see the issue grow. It was realised that there would have to be a major effort to pull together as much information as possible on major criminals as many officers were retiring from the police and taking with them a wealth of knowledge about the crooks and their associates.

In May 1960, with Home Office approval, a Criminal Intelligence Bureau at New Scotland Yard was created. Called C11, its mission was to collate, evaluate and disseminate information regarding organised crime gangs and prominent crooks – known as 'Main Index' or career criminals. Due to the success of the Met initiative it was decided to form similar bureaux in Birmingham, Manchester, Liverpool, Cardiff, Durham and, of course, Glasgow. They had the same terms of reference as the London operation.

In February 1963 two detectives from the City of Glasgow Police were sent to C11 to study their methods and, on their return, the Criminal Intelligence Department was opened in Turnbull Street in Glasgow, in the Central Division and close to police HQ. It provided a service to all the Scottish police forces.

In 1967, Unit Beat Policing was introduced to the City of Glasgow Police. The new system reduced the number of officers on patrol on foot and put them in cars with personal radios. That devalued the 'service' role of the cops and highlighted the crimefighting aspect of the force. The possible loss of access to word on the street from the new initiative meant police had to ensure the flow of good info continued. That led to the establishment of 'collators' – local intelligence units in each of the seven divisions. By 1973 a committee, led by a senior police officer, had been formed to examine the existing systems of gathering intelligence and make suggestions on the structure of a Criminal Intelligence section within the new Strathclyde Police, due to be created two years later.

The department was well established by the time I arrived but it needed some updating. I inherited a card-based intelligence system which was searched to relate a criminal to a crime or a crime to a criminal. The method of analysis relied on memory and continuous updating and had been used for nearly 30 years. Although it had its successes, I reckoned it was time to embrace modern technology. With the help of Strathclyde Regional Council's Department of Information Technology, we used a text retrieval programme to set up SCID (Strathclyde Criminal Intelligence Database) in 1991. That was followed by the CPA (Crime Pattern Analysis) system.

CPA was a boon and helped the department to become a proactive rather than a reactive one, trying to predict what the

207

criminal would do and stop the crime before it happened, rather than having to supply information after the deed was done. There is little doubt that good intelligence in advance of a crime is worth a squad of men after the crime has happened.

'Field intelligence' detective sergeants were introduced and used their wide experience and knowledge of the criminal fraternity to target our Main Index crooks. Together with other dedicated officers we infiltrated most of the gangs and substantially reduced major crime, in particular by hitting teams of armed robbers.

During January 1992, 'Operation Spur', an intelligence-based initiative, was launched to combat a sharp increase in crimes involving firearms. A gun factory was found in the basement of one man's home. He'd been reactivating old and replica firearms and putting a lot of deadly weapons on the streets. We also got word of an AK47-type rifle in Greenock. Good intelligence enabled us to track down the powerful firearm and get it out of the hands of the crooks. At the end of the operation, six months later, an astonishing 656 firearms had been recovered, including semi-automatic assault weapons. Better still, 241 arrests were made.

The role of the Criminal Intelligence branch is to provide intelligence about criminals who ply their trade across divisional boundaries and are involved in serious crime or linked to a series of offences where there is obvious organisation. The intelligence cop has to bring together, in one place, all the information about an individual's dealings and to provide information on anyone who commits or assists with offences. The primary duty is to gather and evaluate information, to develop and send out intelligence and to update and maintain files and computer data as efficiently as possible.

Factual information such as criminal convictions, date of birth and physical description can be gleaned by observation or records held by agencies. Intelligence tends to be suppositional, hearsay and speculative and often unverified, such as suspected activities. So the protection of privacy is important and there has, over many years, been public debate on the right to confidentiality. Privacy has to be weighed against the need to collate vital information to maintain law and order. The Lindop Committee, which reported in December 1978, considered that there should be legislation extending to all automatic handling of data in the UK and many of the recommendations were adopted in the 1984 Data Protection Act.

One problem when I started was that the circulation of intelligence between various government agencies was not very good. Customs and Excise, Immigration, Inland Revenue, Social Security, police and others didn't talk to each other. Info was passed from one to another on the condition that you didn't reveal where you'd got it from. Very few pieces of intelligence were shared through official channels on official forms. We relied on it being exchanged covertly between two people in different agencies who respected and trusted each other.

It was just such a close respect with a senior member of the Inland Revenue in Edinburgh that resulted in my department passing information to them that helped sting Tam McGraw, the Glasgow gangster known as The Licensee.

How McGraw got his nickname is a matter of debate. Some said it was because his wife had a pub, the Caravel, and although her name was on the licence, it was McGraw who was really running the gangsters' haunt. Others allege it was because he was a police informant and in return had a 'licence' to continue his crooked activities unchecked. I don't believe the second explanation is accurate. I certainly did what I could to disrupt McGraw's criminal enterprises.

McGraw was said to have built up a £15 million empire from the sale of drugs and other crime. He spearheaded the notorious Barlanark Team, a successful armed gang that raided post offices and shops in the 1970s.

But despite his activities, McGraw had escaped lengthy jail time. He was sentenced to just 12 months in 1976 for raiding a sub-post office in Bathgate, West Lothian. In 1978 he walked free after a charge of attempted murder of a police officer. He'd hit the cop with his car at a road-block while escaping a robbery. He insisted it was an accident and the accusation was found not proven. In 1983 he got six months for theft, break-ins and opening a lock-fast place. His name, along with others, also came up in connection with the horrific Ice Cream Wars murders of six members of the Doyle family in 1984 – a fatal fire linked to a dispute over ice cream van businesses.

McGraw, who was also in the taxi trade, was very good at getting other people to do his dirty work and we could never get proof of his involvement in anything big. The only thing he was done for around that time was a drink-driving charge. We decided to take the American route and aimed our fire at his tax affairs, echoing the manner in which gangster Al Capone was brought down by the US authorities in the 1930s. I teamed up with my Inland Revenue pal to target McGraw, an unusual move at the time. Information was passed to the taxman from various sources about his dealings, such as property. The Revenue landed McGraw with a bill for tax evasion, reputed to be around £100,000 – and he paid right away. It was probably small change for him.

McGraw's name was then unknown to the public, unlike later when he made regular appearances in the media and even had an official biography published. The operation remained unpublicised in contrast to a subsequent challenge from the taxman that saw McGraw agreeing in 2002 to hand over £300,000.

The cops did have a real go at him in 1998, however. He stood trial accused of masterminding a drug-smuggling operation using a youth football team's minibus to bring in huge quantities of cannabis from the Costa del Sol. Once again, the charge against him was found not proven. The Licensee died from a heart attack in 2007, aged 55.

But criminal intelligence can go wrong, thanks to the reliance on hearsay and speculation. One of my predecessors in the job told me about an incident in the early days of force intelligence, around 1963, involving the well-known gangster Arthur Thompson. The police got word of criminals planning to gather at his home for a 'big job'. So, one Sunday morning, cops staked out the large property in Blackhill, which became known as the Ponderosa. Sure enough, two crooks from London arrived, one of them driving a Rolls-Royce. Soon after four Main Index Glasgow criminals joined them in Thompson's house. Eventually they all emerged on their way to the big job – carrying ladders, paint-pots and brushes. They were there to do up the exterior of Thompson's house! So much for the big crime the cops thought they were on to. But it showed you the respect Thompson was held in that the neds were willing to do his decorating for him.

Arthur Thompson was probably the most publicised Glasgow criminal and, like fellow crook Walter Norval, was given the nickname 'the Godfather' by the press. He was never called that in police circles, however. My role in Criminal Intelligence gave me access to the files on the big villains, including Thompson. While Glasgow had gangsters there was no Mafia-style organised crime in his lifetime.

He was certainly dangerous but any time I encountered him I found the smartly-dressed gangster would always talk civilly and didn't give the cops cause for complaint about his attitude to us. He frequented a pub called the Right Half in George Street and always sat in a seat facing the door so he could see who was coming in.

His main domain was the north of the city but he had contacts in other areas of Glasgow. From the 1950s he maintained links with English underworld figures and arranged for Glasgow villains to go to London to carry out 'contracts' – violent attacks. Thompson was no pussycat and deserved his reputation for violence. He changed the Glasgow crime scene by bringing London villains to the city. They included notorious gangster Billy Hill, who arrived cruising in a Rolls-Royce. Glasgow had not had many links with successful crooks from down south before then.

Thompson ran and frequented illegal gambling dens in the centre of the city in the 1960s and got the equipment – gaming machines and roulette wheels – from the well-known Richardson crime clan, with whom he had the most connections in London. Run by brothers Charlie and Eddie Richardson, the gang had legendary hard man 'Mad' Frankie Fraser as an enforcer and was linked to the gaming machine trade, like Thompson. Thompson was also alleged to have been at or near the scene of two murders in London around that time.

Big Arthur, who modestly claimed he was just the 'doorman' of the Hanover Gaming Club, survived several attempts on his life. In 1966, his mother-in-law, 62-year-old Margaret Johnstone, was killed by a car bomb while she was a passenger in his vehicle. He was hurt but survived. Three brothers, from a family who were feuding with the Thompson clan, were put on trial over the bombing but acquitted. Always having an eye for an earner, Thompson put in a claim to the Criminal Injuries Compensation Board over his injuries. But the hood, who was serving four years for shop-breaking over a clothing theft at the time of the claim, was refused. The Board explained that anyone judged to have provoked a crime could have an award reduced or rejected. Thompson had a total of six convictions by then.

Underworld figure John Friel, who I've mentioned earlier, was said to have been behind an assassination attempt on Thompson in the late 1980s. The Irishman was alleged to have sent one of his countrymen to do the job, said to have been due to a dispute over drugs. The hitman failed in his murderous task because the gun jammed. As the Irish attacker tried to get the weapon to work, it loosed off a round which ricocheted off the ceiling and hit Thompson in the groin. The failed assassin fled and Thompson was said to have booked himself into a private clinic for treatment, claiming a broken drill bit had caused the injury. A couple of years later someone ran Thompson down with a car but he again cheated death.

In 1991, Thompson's son, Arthur junior, was shot dead, but 'the Godfather' died of natural causes two years later despite the various attempts to bring his life to an untimely end. I was among the cops who noticed how Thompson's death sparked a change in the criminal underworld in Glasgow and brought instability to its ranks. Soon various criminals were vying for power and the protection rackets changed from the employment of bouncers at pubs and clubs to private security operations, guarding building sites and other locations.

We're all familiar with the Crimestoppers initiative. It's regularly mentioned in the papers and on TV shows like *Crimewatch*. It allows people to contact the Crimestoppers charity anonymously if they have worries about going direct to the police with information. They can get rewards for their evidence. During my time at Criminal Intelligence the Crimestoppers Scotland programme was put under threat. There was talk of doing away with it but I was determined to see the continuation of what I viewed as a useful initiative. Taking over as coordinator meant I was wearing an extra hat and had more work to do but I reckoned it was worth it.

Crime Stoppers, as it was called when it started in the US in 1976, was brought to the UK by the Community Action Trust, a charity set up as a response by the public and businesses to increased reports of violence. Crimestoppers began in Norfolk in 1983 and by 1988 had expanded to the Met, South Wales and the north of England among others. Moves began to bring it to Scotland and a meeting between interested parties was set up. The scheme needed the participation of the police, the public and the media and approaches were made to the cops in Strathclyde, Lothian and Borders, Central and Fife. STV came on board as the media partner and a 12 month project was agreed between all the groups.

Strathclyde was the base for the new initiative and it was staffed by a detective inspector, a detective sergeant and a

213

detective constable from the Glasgow-based force, aided by a DC from Lothian. DCs from the other forces worked six months each. Crimestoppers Scotland was launched at the STV studios in February 1989 and that first year resulted in 67 arrests and the recovery of over £27,000 of property. But the next year the staff was cut and the DS left. Despite 1990 seeing 51 arrests and nearly £75,000 of property recovered, pressure on the budget continued. In February 1991, the DI was returned to other duties and then, a couple of months later, one of the three DCs left.

I took over Crimestoppers in March 1991 and it was moved into the Criminal Intelligence Department. Around that time the Community Action Trust parent body switched their focus to all crimes, not just violence against the person. Soon after, the *Sunday Post* newspaper joined in, highlighting Crimestoppers appeals in a regular feature in its pages. That was the start of a good relationship I had with the paper, which was to continue after I left the force. The *Post*'s support was a bonus because STV withdrew in June 1991.

That first year I was in charge saw a rise in arrests to 72 after 41 positive calls. That cleared up 50 crimes and over £100,000 of property was recovered. The 400 other positive calls, which didn't have enough info for an arrest, were put in the Criminal Intelligence files for future use.

The public phoned a hotline number, which is still the same today – 0800 555 111 – and could earn up to £5,000 for their tips. When they called they were asked to ring back in ten days to give us a chance to check out their info. Then they'd be told the result. If they wanted a reward – and nearly 80 per cent of callers didn't – they got a code number and were asked to phone back after the next Crimestoppers meeting, at which the value of their tip would be assessed. If it was thought worthy of a reward, they went to a bank of their choice on an agreed day, gave their code number and were handed the cash, which was provided by the business community. A single phone call could earn £100 and twice that year we paid out over £500 for info.

There were more than 4,000 other tips that year which didn't result in anything. Sadly, we were also plagued by malicious calls, often schoolchildren, with over 10,000 of them in 1991. We distributed literature to a range of places and ensured the public were as engaged as possible in the fight against crime in the face of some disillusionment about the criminal justice system and fear of an apparent rising tide of lawlessness.

Amid some criticism from top brass about the perceived low level of positive calls, we re-launched Crimestoppers in September 1992. At that point, I was officially given the title of co-ordinator of Crimestoppers Scotland. We were joined on the day by the actor Mark McManus, who played TV detective Jim Taggart, and Home Affairs Minister Lord Frazer, who both helped publicise some TV appeals. In 1992, Crimestoppers helped to clear up an astonishing seven murders.

At one stage I gave one paper a tasty exclusive – an FBI-style list of Scotland's Most Wanted. After consultation with the Crown Office, I released the mugshots of the men and it made an extremely eye-catching item for the paper.

Members of Neighbourhood Watch schemes at the time were worried about giving info amid fears of reprisals from criminals. Crimestoppers was a great way for people to help the police anonymously. At that time, Strathclyde had an astonishing 12 different hotlines for crime prevention and drug initiatives, so Crimestoppers provided a vital centralised 0800 number that the public could get to know. I'm delighted to see that, more than 20 years on, Crimestoppers is still going strong.

At the end of 1993, after four and a half years at Criminal Intelligence, my time there finished abruptly. It was the closing hours of a Friday and I was looking forward to my weekend off.

But a call from headquarters was to throw me back in to the sharp end of the murder and mayhem.

I was given my new orders. Report first thing on Monday to the CID at D Division, which covered the north and part of the east of Glasgow. At Baird Street Police Office, it turned out, they were very short-staffed. A senior detective on holiday, another one off sick. The same thing with some of the junior staff. They badly needed an experienced detective and I was the man in the frame. So I walked out of the CI department without time for a formal handover to my successor, who was yet to be appointed. I was ready for the fresh challenge as I felt I had done as much as I could in Criminal Intelligence.

There wasn't much time to absorb my new situation. The shrill ring of the phone shattered my Saturday night peace and quiet. In the time-honoured style of TV favourite Taggart, I was told: 'There's been a murdur.' It was in my new patch but I explained that I wasn't due to work there until Monday. No amount of arguing made an impact.

That was the start of a tough few weeks. We had four murders on the go at the same time within the division. Pretty unusual, even for the mean streets of Glasgow. A couple of them were already progressing well by the time I arrived. I didn't get overly involved. If you showed too much interest you'd end up on the inquiry. I already had a bellyful with the fresh cases, which were taken on by me in my new role.

I recall all four were stabbings. One, we didn't manage to pin on anyone despite the locals telling us who was responsible. The other went better. A man had been knifed to death near the infamous Red Road flats in Glasgow. His pal had managed to run away from the attackers but the victim had sight problems and hadn't been able to escape the violence.

A couple of local bad boys were in the frame and I pulled together enough evidence to get them to trial. But in those communities it's very difficult to get folk to give evidence. They can feel intimidated and that's what happened in this case. I had three good witnesses but when push came to shove they clammed up. The trial at the High Court in Glasgow collapsed even though I'd done all I could to bring some justice to the victim's family.

There was plenty more death and mayhem. Later, the body of a murder victim was found on the borderline between my division and the neighbouring one. We were so short of personnel that we were desperate to avoid being landed with the case. There was a big debate about how much of the body was on each side of the divisional border. He was lying on the central reservation of Edinburgh Road. Had he been on the north carriageway he would have been ours. Fortunately, our neighbours became the lead investigators in the murder, which eased the burden on me and my hard-pressed colleagues.

After around a year at Baird Street, I was on the move again – this time to Easterhouse.

Easterhouse has an unenviable reputation for violence throughout Scotland and elsewhere. Having not only worked there but lived there as a teenager, I think it is underserved. Other areas have as much crime.

One day, a beat bobby received a call about a sudden death in a semi-detached house. The lifeless body of an elderly man had been found in his living room by a relative. The constable was faced with a horrific sight and an even worse stench because the man had fallen head-first into his coal fire while trying to use a poker. His roasting head had partly exploded.

He had lived alone for a long time and due to recent ill-health had only used that room. He couldn't get up the stairs to the three bedrooms, the relative explained, and he didn't use the kitchen or dining room on the ground floor. Family members cooked for him and looked after his sanitary needs.

The cop didn't reckon it was a suspicious death, which would have meant calling the CID. But he found something else in the house that led him to alert detectives. Mysteriously, the kitchen and dining room were locked. In the hallway, he could smell something that led him upstairs. Opening one of the bedroom doors, he was met by an amazing sight. There was no furniture in it, only a jungle of cannabis plants! All potted up, there were so many of them that not an inch of the floorboards could be seen.

When I arrived I was stunned to witness a sophisticated watering system had been set up along with timed grow lamps and temperature control devices. I wouldn't have fancied paying their electricity bill! In contrast to the overpowering smell of burning flesh downstairs, the upstairs had a sweet, intoxicating aroma. The other bedrooms and the bathroom were also stuffed with cannabis plants. I'd seen them many times but what was new to me was their cultivation from seed to maturity. This was my first cannabis factory.

After the body had been removed from the living room and the area cleared, we gained entry to the kitchen and dining room. More cannabis plants, including a large one that was the finest specimen we'd seen, were found. It was photographed and the picture was later used during police lectures on drugs.

It was not long before one of the dead man's relatives came forward and took the blame for the horticultural adventure. He'd cynically taken advantage of the rooms that the old man couldn't use to set up his factory. The householder had apparently been totally unaware of the illegal activities going on under his nose, which must have not been too sharp given the strong smell from the plants. Indeed, he'd been delighted that family had been so attentive towards his needs on their regular visits.

The case went to Glasgow Sheriff Court but, disappointingly, was thrown out on a technicality. One of the city's sharper defence lawyers was on the ball, asking me if I had sought a search warrant to look for the cannabis plants. I explained I hadn't because police had gained entry to the house, in the first place, due to a sudden death. However, it was decided we should have had a warrant and the cannabis grower got off, much to my frustration.

After Estonia won its independence in 1991 the country set about revamping its criminal justice system. Their eyes turned to Scotland for some advice and they wanted to see Easterhouse during a state-sponsored tour of the country. I was delighted to welcome two ladies from their prosecution service to Glasgow. One of them spoke perfect English and during their stay my wife and I invited them to dinner at our home. Our bi-lingual visitor painted a bleak picture of their former life under Soviet control and said she was looking forward to the development of the new, free Estonia. Although money was tight, her country had decided to upgrade its legal system to something similar to Scotland.

She was one of the country's top prosecutors but her salary was very low compared to ours. She hoped to take home some presents to her young children as they were cheaper here, so I told her about the Wednesday weekly market, where toys and other goods were sold at the Easterhouse shopping centre car park. Our visitor was obviously a learned lawyer from the higher strata of the former Communist country. But she was wide-eyed with amazement after she returned from her visit to the market. She was intrigued by the teeming streets. 'Why are all these people out during the day, spending so much money?' she inquired. She was especially puzzled that so many men had free time.

I explained that a fair few of them were probably unemployed so didn't have anywhere else to be on a Wednesday morning. Coming from a country that wasn't exactly flush, she was stunned. 'But how do they afford to buy these things?' she demanded. I told her some of them were on benefits – getting their money from Social Security.

She continued to ponder this remarkable situation. I don't think her country had a similar welfare system. It seemed to her that these out-of-work people were paid more by the state than some hard-working folk in her nation earned in a full-time job. She was delighted when I told her the Social Security recipients were known, in local parlance, as the 'Soshy people'.

The impact of what she'd seen obviously stuck with her during her visit. At the end of her two-day tour, she thanked me for my hospitality and, with an impish smile, announced, 'I am going to request a transfer from Estonia to Scotland. I would like to become a Soshy person!' Obviously life on the dole in Glasgow looked like a cushier option than prosecuting crime as capitalism took hold in her burgeoning nation.

20

THE BABY CLUE, THE SNOWBALL KILLER
AND TIME TO GO

There was a big rammy in an Easterhouse street. One man came out of his house and got caught up in the stramash although he was a decent type of character, and not involved in the initial fracas. I recall it was around the time the film *Braveheart* hit our screens in 1995. Among the weapons getting wafted about was a big sword, not exactly a claymore, but enough to later put me in mind of Mel Gibson's William Wallace swinging a blade around. The man was stabbed at some point either by the sword or another weapon among those being brandished at the scene.

After the ambulance had rushed him to the Royal Infirmary, I sent a team down to check on his condition. Being in charge, I would be directing the investigation but not faced with tasks like door-to-door inquiries and attending post-mortems.

Sadly, the victim died. In the interim a woman got in contact with me. Her partner had gone outside during the row. She had stayed inside their house during the trouble and had seen police cars and the ambulance as the mayhem subsided. She wasn't sure if her man had done something wrong and run off to avoid getting caught. All she knew was that he hadn't come home yet. I realised she was probably the other half of our victim.

Right away I got someone to bring us the personal items belonging to the man who'd died. There were things like a ring, a watch, a card from a business. She studied them and identified them as her partner's.

She looked at me in confusion. Did we have her man in custody, she wondered? There was no doubt the dead man was her partner. I swallowed hard as I began trying to break the dreadful news as gently as possible. Taking my time as I built to the sad revelation, I said, 'As you know there was an incident outside your house. Your partner ran out to see what was happening. I have to tell you he was struck by a weapon of some sort and had to be taken to hospital.'

As her eyes widened, I continued in best police-speak, 'I have to inform you that he has succumbed to his injuries.' I braced myself for her emotional outburst but it came in a form I wasn't anticipating. No tears or hysterics. A broad smile crossed her face and she stood up with a sigh of relief. 'Does that mean he will be alright, then?' she beamed.

My heart sank as I realised she'd misinterpreted the phrase, taking it to mean that he was recovering from the wounds. I kicked myself, thinking I'd been a right wally using a word like 'succumbed' in the circumstances. It was inappropriate but perhaps I'd been trying to lessen the impact for both of us by choosing a gentler phrase than, 'He has died.'

I felt so bad for that woman as, in clearer language, I had to dash her hopes within seconds of them being falsely raised. It made me think about how I handled these things in future when dealing with ordinary folk who didn't need to be bamboozled by big words they wouldn't normally hear.

Another memorable example of a term being misunderstood came earlier in my career in CID. It also involved a man dying of stab wounds. His heartbroken family were gathered round him as he lay in agony, waiting for medical help. A group of men had forced their way into his house and stabbed him repeatedly before running off.

With no idea what to do to ease his torment, the family remembered hearing the well-known phrase 'to rub salt in the wound'. So that's exactly what they did! They thought it was a handy tip on what to do to ease the pain of a deep gash. How wrong they were!

The shock of the stinging salt eating into his bloody wounds must have taken its toll on the already weakened man. He died in agony. It was such an unusual story that it was the talk of the steamie.

You could never tell how people would react to news of a relative's death. Some would be stony-faced, others would be distraught, but one decided to shoot the messenger in a dramatic way. After a sudden death, I got a phone call saying a young man had walked into the police station at Shettleston. He was a family member, who we were expecting to identify the body, and he explained he'd been told the police wanted to see him.

He obviously hadn't had the full picture from his upset family, so I went to see him. I took him into a quiet office and tried to break it to him as gently as possible. But as I began to explain how his relative had died, his face indicated that he had no idea at all he was there to identify a body. I realised he just thought the polis wanted to speak to him about something. He'd presumably been told to go to station so he could be updated there.

Sometimes you handle it right in these situations and sometimes it goes wrong. When I told him of the death he lost control. He burst into tears then began to rage against the dreadful news. Before I realised what was going on, he picked up a chair and smashed me over the head with it.

Fortunately, I'd been able to brace myself and it wasn't a solid piece of furniture so I wasn't knocked out or badly hurt. Assaulting a cop is a serious offence but I took pity on him, appreciated he'd acted out of wild instinct after being driven to distraction by the tragedy. I don't think he knew what he was doing. He just lashed out at me because I was there. I didn't charge him. It often struck me that murder blighted the lives of people like those above, who were least able to cope with it – the poor, uneducated and underprivileged. I'm sure it's the same for others but it is the poor end of society that bears the brunt of crime.

In those latter stages of my career, I would ponder the many killings I'd seen. Although many like a good murder mystery on the TV it's never like *Inspector Morse* or Agatha Christie's books. It's not glossed in glamour and intrigue. More like the Sweeney, if I had to say any of those shows were realistic. During many murder probes, I saw folk shot, stabbed and strangled. But, unlike the fictional world of murder, where clever scheming leads to baffling deaths, I reckon only a small percentage of them were premeditated. The average homicide takes place in a banal and brutal flash of rage. It's murder most foul but not malice aforethought.

Usually the killer and victim knew each other, which could make our job easier, at least. Sometimes the pettiest of reasons led to fatal attacks. But it was always sad and sordid.

It's not often that a baby helps solve a wave of crimes. But that's what happened when we had a problem in Easterhouse in early 1996 – the highest level of housebreakings in the whole division. Someone was climbing up drainpipes to get into homes and steal property. We had no sightings of the intruder, no fingerprints and no clues. Nearly 20 raids were recorded over a short period of time and the amount stolen was rising alarmingly. Most of the items taken were small – money or jewellery – but some larger property such as electrical goods and clothes had been reported stolen.

I was determined to stop the crimewave and organised a meeting with Easterhouse's finest detectives and uniformed officers. They were soon fully briefed on the spate of house-breakings and the long list of property stolen from folk in our area. We blitzed the usual places where nicked goods were sold but found nothing. All the local resetters were also visited but that didn't take us any further.

More homes were hit by the sneaky thief but once again he'd slipped in without leaving any prints or other forensic clues. This was getting frustrating. One of the local councillors was the next victim and, to make things worse, his chain of office was among the items stolen. The pressure on us from above to solve the string of break-ins increased now that such an upright member of society had been hit. Local jewellery stores and pawnbrokers were told to be on the lookout for the councillor's chain but we got no word.

I decided to bring in plainclothes cops to help us out, hoping they'd catch the rone pipe bandit in the act. We knew the crook usually waited until the house lights went out and climbed in after the occupants were in bed. Extra beat patrols were put in place until 2am each night but again the elusive housebreaker slipped through the net.

Time to get nasty with the local criminal fraternity. They either knew who was doing it and weren't telling us or they didn't have a clue. We had to find out which. We made our presence felt to cramp the style of every known chancer, even the wide boys selling contraband cigarettes in the local market. Every bar was visited and the publicans were told clearly that the police wouldn't stop turning up at their door until the housebreaker was named. They all got the message but none of them could tell us anything. The local underworld figures insisted they had no information and I came to believe them because their activities were being severely impeded by the police operation.

It seemed our man was an outsider who was coming into the area to ply his trade. We'd hoped that by then all the hours of action would have come to fruition as criminals are territorial and don't like anyone encroaching on their patch. There were

225

more robberies and still no answers. We alerted the local papers, which highlighted the run of break-ins on their doorstep. The criminal intelligence files, both local and at force level, proved unhelpful.

Break-in followed break-in. Now it was time for even more drastic measures. More extra patrols were put on the streets and the local crooks were left tearing their hair out as they couldn't get us off their backs.

The most worrying aspect of this type of criminal was what he might have done after he'd entered a house. What would have happened if the occupants had woken up while he was in there or returned while he was raiding an empty home? That could have been very traumatic for victims and even have led to violence. I remember once attending a housebreaking where the thief had climbed up a rone pipe and managed to remove rings from the fingers of a sleeping woman. She was so terrified when she realised what had happened that she didn't want to stay in her home any longer.

I regularly put in late hours to help with the investigation. I undertook Crime Pattern Analysis to work out if there was a particular day when the offences would occur or a favourite street that was targeted. It appeared to be completely random although weekdays were most common, suggesting someone was short of money before his benefits were paid on a Thursday. So we were all out on Wednesdays, including me.

Then an unusual call came in one night about 11pm. A woman claimed she had heard a baby crying loudly in her back court. It sounded unlikely. Perhaps it was an animal or a whining car alarm. But when an officer got to the scene he heard the wean, bawling by then because he had been on his own for a while. The six-month-old boy was tucked up in his pram but there was no sign of a parent anywhere.

We made sure the baby was quickly taken back to the station to keep warm. It wasn't the environment for a little one and we weren't well set up as a kindergarten. Arrangements were made for the abandoned tot to be looked after by social services while we hunted for mum and dad.

The same night, at 2am, we finally got our lucky break regarding the thief. A couple and their 25-year-old son returned to their flat after a night out to find a man robbing the place. He'd shinned up the rone pipe – our thief's favourite MO – to get in. The family were especially outraged because the householder's elderly mother was asleep in the spare bedroom, having turned in about midnight. Fortunately, she was unharmed.

The same couldn't be said for the intruder after the family had taken their revenge by assaulting him. They'd spent a while sorting him out before calling the cops to take him away. He was hardly going to complain about getting his just desserts, although he was insistent that his leather jacket had been stolen from him during his unexpected detention.

We took him to the station for an interview but he was saying nothing. As we'd suspected, he wasn't a local and none of us recognised him. He refused to give us his name or tell us where he lived. He was a typical arrogant criminal who obviously felt no remorse over the innocent victims he'd violated by robbing their homes. It looked like it was going to be a long night.

Then, suddenly, a look of shock came across his face and his cocky attitude changed. He began to panic and screamed, 'Where's ma wean? I left him in the back court in his pram!' He'd obviously forgotten about junior among all the drama of his capture. Now we had a window of opportunity. We told him we would search for the baby – but he'd have to tell us why he'd abandoned the tot so late at night in that location. He had no idea the wee boy was already safe.

So he finally began to talk, explaining why the baby was mixed up in the whole thing. Little could we have guessed the sweet-looking family picture that was behind the crimes. The man and his girlfriend had taken to walking round the area, innocently pushing the pram carrying their young baby. Nothing suspicious about that to spark the interest of any eagle-eyed cops on patrol to spot vagabonds.

As she stood rocking junior in the pram, keeping a lookout, he'd nip into the darkness of a garden or back court and look for a way in to a house or flat. He'd usually shin up a drainpipe in rat-like fashion. Then he'd pop back out with his ill-gotten gains and hide them in the pram, which provided an ideal place to stash the gear.

Unsurprisingly, they were both drug addicts. The happy family unit was broken up when she got the jail for other offences and was sent to Cornton Vale women's prison. But he had continued his pram perambulations in the evenings, making sure he looked like a doting dad rather than a cunning crook. He'd park the baby carriage with the tot inside and make his lightning attack on a property.

All the crimes were cleared up and most of the property was recovered through the information he gave us. The local criminals certainly breathed a sigh of relief because the heat was off and we were delighted that the housebreaking figures dropped back to almost zero.

One of the most mindless murders I ever dealt with was the case of a knifeman who stabbed a young man to death – for throwing snowballs. The victim launched the missiles at a couple of yelping dogs on the balcony of a home in Cranhill in 1996. The owner of the mongrels didn't take kindly to this. He raced downstairs and dashed outside in a rage to confront the man, 24-year-old Martin Siegerson.

John McGeechan had a carving knife in his hand and plunged it into the victim's heart. The dying man was comforted by a local girl while he fought for breath but witnesses said the ambulance had taken him away without its siren sounding, meaning it was too late to help Martin.

I was head of CID at Easterhouse so I raced to the scene with a colleague to find out what had happened and who was responsible. I had no stab vest to protect me from the potentially-crazed knifeman. After speaking to witnesses, it became obvious that we needed to speak to McGeechan. We climbed the stairs to his flat and knocked several times on the door. No answer. We cautiously entered the house and found our man in the kitchen. At the sink, he appeared to be doing the dishes. Strange behaviour for someone who had just killed, I reckoned. But then I spotted one of the kitchen utensils he'd been cleaning. A large knife! Looked like he'd been doing his best to cover up the crime.

Our man was in a highly-agitated state as we led him into the living room, content that he didn't have any other weapons on him. By this time in my career, I had become almost anaesthetised to bloody murder, even a bizarre killing like this. So we went through our procedure, arresting McGeechan and taking him to the station. I recall he was calm and compliant by then, apparently accepting of what had happened.

Unemployed Martin had apparently been making the regular trip from his flat to his mother's house when the deadly encounter happened. He'd often popped round for breakfast. He'd been playing snowballs with local kids when the dogs had caught his eye and mayhem had ensued.

McGeechan, in his thirties, was described to us as a loner who had become a virtual recluse. He lived with his elderly mum and rarely ventured outside except to walk his beloved dogs. He was said to have terrified some of the locals and to have previously threatened people. The idea of someone teasing his pets, however playfully, had obviously driven him to the edge. Although he'd known his victim and had played football with Martin, he'd showed no mercy.

As we investigated, the community fought to come to terms with its loss, baffled that anyone could have died in such a senseless way. The spot where he'd fallen was covered with

Celtic scarves. Martin's family and friends were joined by more than 300 mourners as they packed a local church to pay their last respects. There were tears as the popular young man's coffin was carried past. Many broke down when they saw his coffin. A display of flowers spelled out his nickname, 'Siegy'.

His mum and his sisters described him as a lovely lad who had helped look after his nieces, taking them to nursery and school. So it must have been difficult for them to take when McGeechan admitted a reduced charge of culpable homicide instead of murder. Martin's mother couldn't hide her rage in court and threw her rosary beads at the man who'd so cruelly snuffed out her son's life. The 'Snowball Killer' was given ten years.

In retrospect, we were stupid to have rushed to such a dangerous scene without armed back-up. But that was how it was done in those days. We were unarmed and had no stab vests so we could have put ourselves in harm's way if our suspect had been prone to another crazed, violent attack. We were perhaps lucky to get away without being injured. That wouldn't happen in the modern police service. I'm glad to see that the health and safety of officers means none of them would find themselves in that situation now.

I saw McGeechan's face crop up in the press again in 2008 when he was convicted of killing another man. He'd served six years before being released on licence, then been called back to jail for three years after committing a minor crime. He'd then moved to Maybole in Ayrshire, where, in 2006, another innocent had become a victim of his lawless blade. He'd attacked Ahmjid Ismail, whose family ran a local grocer's shop. Ahmjid, aged 34, who had learning difficulties, was on his own in charge of the shop when McGeechan burst in and demanded money. As the terrified shopkeeper tried to phone for help, McGeechan stabbed him eight times in the face, neck and body.

It struck me as sad and poignant that, on the day of the murder in November 2006, Ahmjid was minding the shop because his parents were away at a passing-out parade for his brother, who had just finished training as a policeman.

Cowardly McGeechan fled the shop and dumped his blood-stained jacket and the knife in bushes. The horrific attack was captured on the shop's CCTV cameras, which was obviously a big help for the cops on the case.

At the High Court in Edinburgh, judge Lady Clarke told McGeechan he was 'wicked' and said he posed a high risk of danger to the public. She noted he'd shown no mercy and used a knife repeatedly against a defenceless victim. Despite his terrible injuries, he'd tried to summon help, she pointed out. But brutal McGeechan stole the phone, taking away his only means of getting assistance.

This time the Snowball Killer was jailed for a minimum of 20 years. Not surprisingly, his previous victim's relatives said he should have still been in jail at the time of his second killing. Martin's mother said her son's life had been worth more than ten years, and it was hard to disagree with her. She hoped McGeechan would rot in hell, she said.

So she and her family would have cared little when they saw press reports later that year that McGeechan had got a taste of his own medicine in prison. It was claimed the double killer had been stabbed 17 times with the bottom of a smashed coffee jar in Shotts Prison in Lanarkshire.

McGeechan was said to be scarred for life in the assault with staples and stitches in his face and body after being treated in Crosshouse Hospital in Kilmarnock. It was claimed he was a heroin addict and was attacked as he slept on a bunk bed in his cell. Obeying the prison code, he hadn't revealed who'd cut him up, it was said. There would have been no shortage of suspects among the inmates who were aware of his cruel killings.

It looked like we had an attempted assassination on our hands. In a pleasant, modern housing estate near Easterhouse, a drug dealer opened his front door to find a man standing there aiming a handgun. The hitman opened up with three shots before casually walking away. The victim was shot at close range in the frightening attack, which happened in late 1996.

The bid to kill the dealer failed and he was rushed to hospital for treatment. One bullet had hit him in the arm, the others were embedded in the floor and the banister on the stair. I arrived to start an attempted murder inquiry and, having surveyed the scene, went to see the shaken victim at the Royal Infirmary, where he'd been patched up.

I wasn't confident that he'd talk to me, given his line of work. But he surprised me by telling me everything, claiming a very prominent gangster – one of our Main Index criminals – was his assailant. The shooting was a result of a drug deal that had gone wrong and the pusher gave me a full statement outlining the events that had led up to the murder bid.

It was unusual for a gangster to give such a graphic statement against a fellow criminal but I was in no doubt he was telling the truth and determined to see his attacker prosecuted. However, there were no other witnesses and we couldn't find any forensic evidence at the crime scene apart from the recovered bullets.

A police guard was mounted at the victim's bedside until he was discharged and placed in a safehouse. I called at the fiscal's office with my report, requesting a warrant to arrest the gunman. But she refused on the grounds that there wasn't enough corroboration of the allegations. Her best suggestion was that I should detain the wanted man for six hours, as Scots Law allows. But no criminal of any note ever speaks to the police during a detention, so I wasn't keen on that idea. I wanted him locked up so potential witnesses could feel safe and brave enough to come forward with information. I also knew the suspect was now staying in England – causing cross-border hassle over any detention move.

I managed to get a search warrant to try to recover the gun or other evidence relevant to the case. Several houses were raided, ensuring a number of the gangster's associates were alerted to what he was wanted for. Later, information came in to say that he was back in Glasgow. Then we got a call telling us he was in a house in the east of the city – and was tooled up.

With my search warrant, I was ready for action. But we needed armed support. By then the days of CID officers carrying firearms were gone and the only way to get armed back-up was with the approval of the senior uniformed officer in the division where our suspect was holed up. He could assess the situation and call out uniformed firearms cops if he judged it necessary – but they were not on duty 24 hours a day. He quizzed me closely on my target. What type of gun did he have? Where in the house was he? How many others were in the building with him? I couldn't give him definitive answers but assured him my informant was tried and tested.

By then it was well past midnight and I wanted the raid to kick off after 2am. The boys were in place and ready to go. But my plans were scuppered as the senior cop refused to call out the firearms team. I had hoped he would have at least agreed to send an armed officer to cover us while we surrounded the house, waiting for the suspect to leave. But even that was too much for him to sanction. Feeling angry and let down, I had no option but to withdraw the detectives from the area. The following day saw sparks fly between the CID and the uniformed branches over the way the incident had been handled.

It was a prime example of how things were altering within the force – and not for the better, in my opinion. It came not long after another example of the changed ways. I had charged a man with murder in the Easterhouse area and assumed he was still inside awaiting trial. Looking out of my office window one day, I saw him strolling along the street. Normally bail was not given for such a serious crime and, if it was, the senior investigating officer would be informed by the court of the decision. I had not been updated and, more worryingly, I doubt if the witnesses had either. They would have got a fright if they'd encountered the man in the street.

Perhaps the whole thing was a clerical error! But it pointed to the way things would go in the years ahead. These days, the accused seem to get bail for murder charges more often than ever. The two incidents showed me how the system was changing and it made me think about my future. Maybe it was time to hand in my warrant card.

Having reached the age of 50, it was time to consider my future outwith the police. I could stay until the age of 60 or carry on for a few more years, perhaps until I was 55. But by that point in my career I had been involved in investigating almost every crime in the book – and I had qualified for a good pension. Crime was becoming repetitive for me. Times were changing and I didn't like some of the new ways but could do little to reverse them.

I'd worked some of the poorest and most challenging areas while in uniform and been in all the departments I'd wanted to be a part of in the CID. During a moment of reflection, I tried to count all the murder inquiries I had attended. I recalled how the late 1970s had been a particularly busy and brutal time as Strathclyde experienced more murders than Northern Ireland at the height of their Troubles.

I'd served nine years straight in the squads and been on the spot when they'd been called to all the major incidents of the time. On two heartbreaking occasions, I remembered, I'd seen a victim die in front of me as we waited for an ambulance to speed to the scene. On some murder inquiries the squad were called in days after the crime to battle for clues in the toughest of cases. I counted nearly 230 murders over my career.

At that point I was still happy being a cop but could see myself becoming disgruntled as change increasingly took effect. Like all detectives before me, I thought I had seen the best of the job. I'd learned from hugely-experienced men who, once they'd been appointed to the CID, never left. I was now one of the small group of detectives who had not been uniform since joining the CID. The new thinking was that more interchange between CID and uniform was a good idea. Some were happy with the idea of only doing short spells as a detective to enhance the CV.

I tendered my resignation without fuss and calculated that, including time-off owed, my last day would be at the end of December 1996. The day before the day I thought would never come, two of my colleagues, good detectives, suggested that I not take my car to work on my last day and they would arrange a lift for me. Expecting one of them to pick me up in their own car, I answered the door at 8am. I was surprised to see a man in uniform, who asked for me by name. He wasn't a police officer. He was a chauffeur, with a Rolls-Royce to take me on my final journey to the Easterhouse Police Office in style. Inside the Roller was a bottle of champagne and a cigar – a nice touch from a great bunch of detectives.

It was a great ending to a long and happy career.

21

EPILOGUE: THE MISSING WIFE

As I told you at the start of this book, I became a private detective for a while after leaving the job. I also kept in touch with the *Sunday Post* newspaper, which had been so helpful in publicising Crimestoppers while I was in charge of that initiative. I began working with the *Post* as a consultant on crime stories and was soon thrown back into a murder case.

The name of Nat Fraser is now among the most well-known in Scottish criminal history. The Elgin businessman has been convicted of his wife Arlene's murder – twice. In 2003 he was jailed for a minimum of 25 years for getting a hitman to kill and dispose of Arlene in 1998. The body of the 33-year-old mother-of-two, who'd been planning to divorce Fraser, has never been found. But after a long appeal process, Fraser had his conviction quashed in 2011 and was released while he awaited his retrial.

He was found guilty of the killing for a second time in May 2012 and sentenced to a minimum of 17 years. He quickly appealed the verdict, as he had done with his previous conviction. I'm one of the few, outwith legal circles, who has met and spoken to Fraser about his wife's disappearance. At the time, less than two months after Arlene Fraser vanished, her husband wasn't officially a suspect. I travelled north with a *Sunday Post* reporter and met the Grampian Police officers investigating the case.

They were happy to allow us to quiz Fraser about the mystery. As we greeted him at his bustling fruit and veg business I knew there was a strong chance I was looking into the eyes of a killer. But I didn't know then if I'd just shaken the hand that had passed a wad of notes to a hitman, hired to snuff out Arlene's life while Fraser ensured his alibi by joking with customers on his delivery round and making a phone call at the exact time she disappeared.

As we questioned him, images of his wife's lifeless body must have raced through his brain – but his eyes were dead too. He was emotionless, chillingly unconcerned. A strange smile played across his lips and his replies seemed stilted. He appeared to me to be a man who'd detached himself from the situation.

Unlike the portly, grey-haired figure that later appeared in court, back then Fraser was slim and dark-haired. He joined in jovial banter with colleagues, looking nothing like a man concerned by the police's unspoken interest in him amid the gossip he'd killed his wife. I was surprised detectives had been so accommodating in arranging an interview. They'd put in a cheery phone call to Fraser and told him it was a good idea he spoke out.

At that time the police were saying they reckoned Fraser was nothing more than a small-time crook, allegedly involved in bootlegging. That could have been a tactic to get him to let his guard down, but maybe they were taken in by him at that early stage. But it was easy to see why suspicion was pointing his way. There was no sign of the charming chap whose cheeky patter had ladies eating out of the palm of his hand.

It was an uneasy experience as I listened to him paint a picture of himself as a devoted father who was the victim of hurtful slurs. 'I've been asked many times if I had something to do with it. The answer is no,' he told us in a quiet, monotone voice. 'If she's out there, I'd ask her to come home for the sake of the bairns.'

What his children, Jamie, then ten, and Natalie, then five, didn't know about their devoted dad was that he was blackening their mother's name in a calculated offensive against the rumours about him. He told anyone who'd listen that Arlene was a bad mother, who stayed out all night. Speaking to us, it was a very different picture. He said he constantly turned the mystery over in his mind and worried about Arlene. He wanted to stay friends after the divorce that had been planned before her disappearance.

'You hold on to the hope she might have gone off by choice. After all, some of her clothes were missing from the house,' he tried to convince us, in the knowledge her coat had been burned along with the car bought to transport her body. In a cynical ploy, days before our meeting, he'd put up a £10,000 reward for information. But the man who'd killed to avoid a costly divorce knew his money was safe.

Fraser insisted, 'People who don't know me will make up their own minds. People who know me know I'm not involved.' But it was one of those who knew him best who was to condemn him years later. His friend Hector Dick went on to reveal the whole gruesome story in court as a prosecution witness, claiming Fraser had told him he'd paid a hitman £15,000 to kill Arlene.

'I see her every day,' Fraser told us, as he related imagined sightings of his wife amid his fake concern for her. Desperately trying to draw an emotional response, my reporter pal asked what he'd do if Arlene walked round the corner safe and well. He pondered a scenario an innocent man would have thought about over and over – but to Fraser it was an impossibility he'd never had to consider. As he glanced at the racks of produce in his warehouse, he stunned me with the coldness of his reply. 'I'd give her a nice basket of fruit,' he smiled.

We hadn't told Fraser I was an ex-cop. As far as he was concerned, I was just another reporter. But I left with a gut feeling, drawn from years of experience, that he was involved.

I'd worked on scores of murder investigations and sat opposite dozens of killers and knew what I was looking at. 'That's your man,' I told my colleague confidently. Two trials confirmed my copper's instinct had remained intact long after I'd left the job I loved.